SALAMANDER'S WOOL

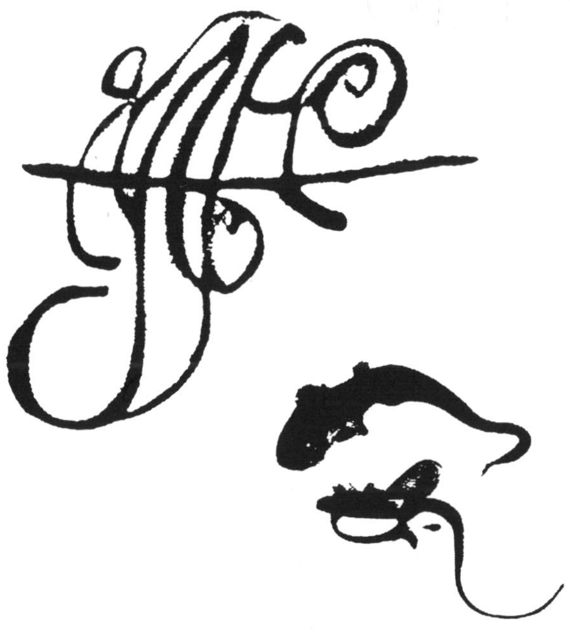

ARGOT OF AZOTH

purifyour lairvoyant
keep the fire moist

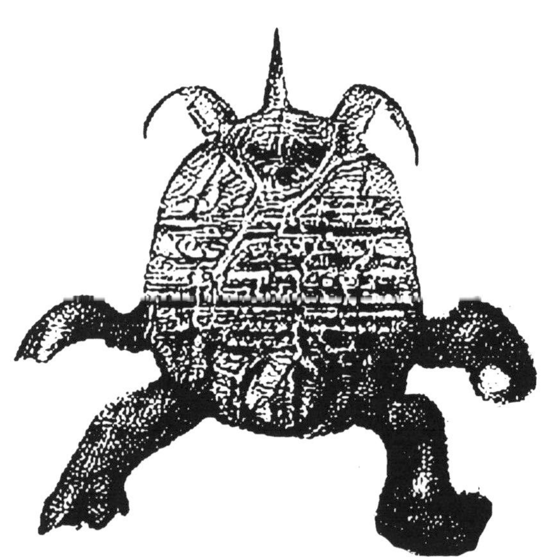

SALAMANDER'S WOOL

HERMAPHRODITE of REANIMATING DEW
CHILDREN of the ABYSS
INFANT and the HYDROLITH
SALIVA of CERBERUS
MARROW of the WAND
a BOOK of GOD is a LUCIFER
REVOLVINGALPHABET of REANIMATING DEW
ALCHEMYTHOPOESIS
OTHER WATER GODS
LABYRINTH! Replace These Gods!
RADISH! Replace These Gods!
EVEN CHAOS SETS ALTARS
AZOTHISTLE~SIFTER • QUEENS of the
CIRCULATING LIBRARY

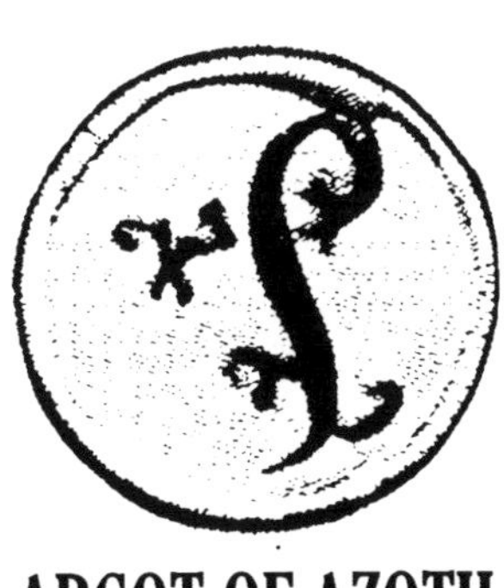

ARGOT OF AZOTH

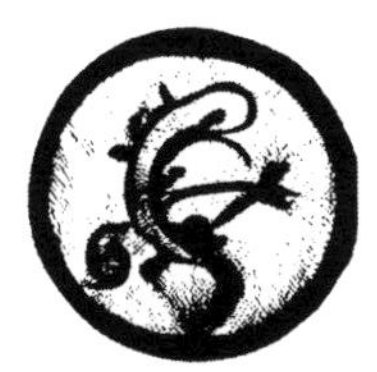

HERMAPHRODITE OF REANIMATING DEW

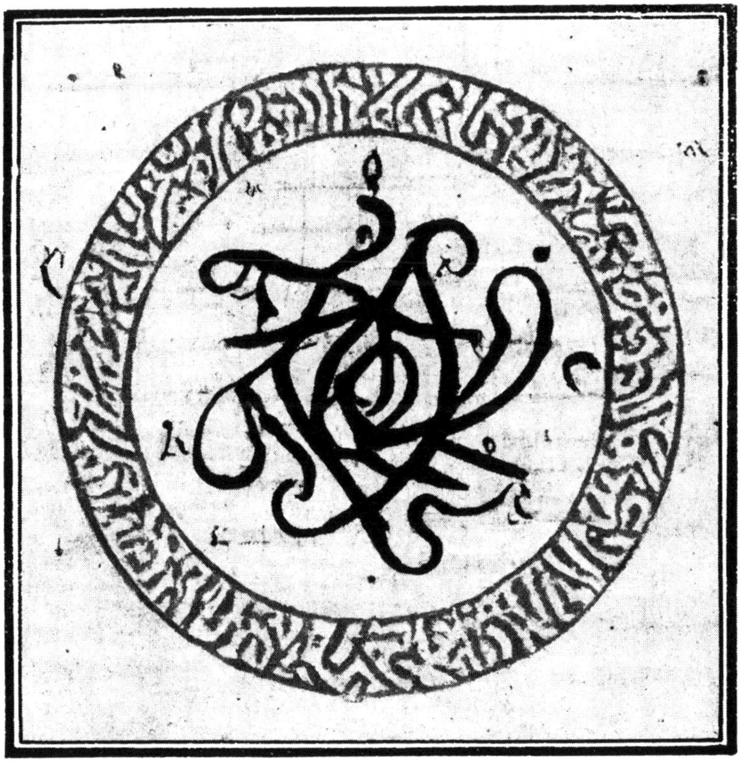

---

the words are whispered
in the OATH
OF THE DRAGON
simplenough
yet
Dragon in the vulgar tongue
is a feeling
not a word

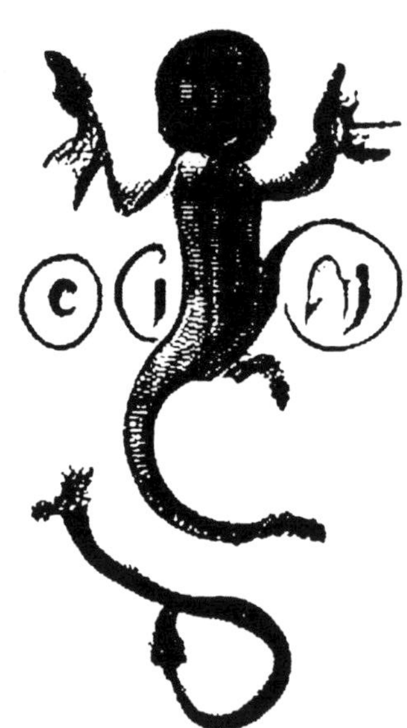

| proem |
○ we are between light-bringers ○

Opus
Azoth
handwritten
Infinigrammaton
aEpigrammata ~
Omnigrammaton
Azoth
A and Z of the gods
unbind
in the ash of things
Azoth
A points upward
Elijah's Inscription
biscriptal
Azoth
becompossible flame
an Argot of Azoth
Azothistle-sifter

revolvessel
labyrintheir
revolvinglight
the Alchemical shadow
a Magnum Opus
or,
an opera minimus
of true spiritual burns
an Alchemistake
a coppercipher
praying scriptomantis
with scripture aflower
a dew
in the humidity
of the secret mentioning
the unglyphable bliss
of syllabic sorcery

upon a thousand
aeons of the turtle

the Light-mare —

LIGHT DRIPS
SPARK HANGS
FROM ABOVE
THE SERPENT
*Spark = SPIRIT HANGS
FROM BELOW
THE PRIMORDIAL

~ *this is*
between
transcriptions ~

why the dew of the spirit
corporally disappears
until its approximating renew

and of alembics
and their essences :
WATER
SWEATS PROFUSELY
° COPPER DIVINING ROD
lifts
and the glass asks
for gathered dew
from a crepuscular dawn

an inscription of invisible ink
of ever-burning literature
write for 100 days
then place the *ribbon in the book*
Omnigrammata
autopoietic Scriptomancy
and a Reviving Codex ~
the birth of letters
a poem-writing them down
syllabic sorcery
where the symbols matter
the two-letter spell
of intra-sundiaeval worship
Heliotaxis

and the six-moons-embrace*
to reflect on the secret
of two radishes
[kept underground]

lone are the guides
moontorch-gentle
into the Quinterior
quest-lust in their ember-cadabra
in search of
phosphorescripture
clairvvoyantly
hymns splendoubtedly
aphthonged
clairaudiently

innerHEAT
the microcosmic
cauldron and stove
where the involuntary whispering
of the dew-harvest
meets
the wand of the grimoires
found
on the axis
of the ladder
where the words are
PREPARED FOR GOD
the thousand-named
serpent of letters
in the TREE-ALPHABET
palimpses,
then slumps into the bonfire

pyroglyphic homonculi
in the ashes
of the
TREE-ALPHABET
the sun's copper book
it happears —
the poetry of purify
a spell-binding book
Spagyric *Sangraal*
or this
otheralphabet / hiddententional

in its
inhaling and exhaling

two other manuscripts
kept on a simmer
I had eaten
the sacred writings

we Alchymistook
the talisman
for the philosophy
are these blossoms
in the Maze of Heaven
or just Knots in the Gateway
unless appears a cipher
in her emblem,
I will be found in a poem

and you'd rather book ?
it's signacula
between transcribblers
of the navel-gaze
Indecipherers !
author-demons !
with arcane names
for the words
words are impure
sometimes demolish meaning
Demolisher !
the gods
are manifest
Manifester !
unmanifest : ~~disappear~~
UNMANIFESTER !

I am the *Sickle* towards
the *Ignitingcenter*
the blight inItself
*alchemself
UNINTERPRETER !

upon an
altar
of
Letters

appears an omniliteral
'riddle of clairvvoyance
the myſtery
of Divine Illusion
old Scribbler
of Signification *herself*
in the ſpaces below :

REMEMBERER !
FORGOTTER !
Othermaphroditic Hymns
to the hylic protoplaſt
secreturned and sexualigned

Sigil-eater
in an
Hermaphroditic Cavern
orchid comb-jelly
urchin choral-magic
dew-tongued
thiſtled, gently
two-tree female
Oracle-Satyr of a
Totem of Light
\
demon of the Circle
Sigvil in the Sigvil
a golden thorn
among mortal alphabets
| Vajra |
hereby the Diamond
twenty-seven letters
of the Diamond
the Hydromancy
of all letters
in the Demon Fire
toadſtongues Hydromancy
the dropletter horns
of the *dovble vv*

a lightning
in the firſt sigvil
cryptic handwriting
**zigzags in the ſtriations*
fire-writing
fulgurite

up six riddle-streams
of Ophidian current
volcanic soils
sprouting-chaos *beginnings do not matter*
serpents grew tongues
and sudden perceptive gifts
to soak up their words
between floods
and a Worm
became a River
wonderscending
up, up,
ANIMATING ALPHABETS
nesting shedding slithering
we snakes
with spellbinding alphabets
swim up
the River Wheelzebub
secluded
and noble waters
hidden within
the snake's word-forest
cave-keeping
dizzyingdaemons
of the sacredsmallocalypse
solar snake
originally unconscious
error-charmer amongst
the writing-serpent's mistakes
to become
desensitized
to the venom
and to nurture
a serpent-daemonstanding
of hidden heliographic messages
in the crooked serpent
of the letters

hiddenhead of the snake
likely to disappoint
upon deeper cult in-access
the head
withought cognition
our snake
on the water there,
reflecting
the sun’s light

language
only sparkles
when we see the words

we see the words

† Occulligraphy †

â ã å ä
written by jugglers

† Occulligraphy †

ú ù î ì ò ô ç æ ù ú ë ì
written by jugglers

where younger words
pair and mate
we are pruning and composing
zero famous works
abecedarian
nature's vital A
Omnigrammarian
Aleph-nought inversion
dues absconditus —
god hidden in matter
hapax legomenon —
word
that only appears once
ONOMASTICA
reported
by the scribes
of god's booklore
Orpheus also we read, yet
Orpheus did not read
Dionysus did not read
our illiterate forebearers
tossed the Manuscript's ashes
through the window
ouroboros
a curious walk through
the book
of the door
PREFACE
discovered without language
| nevertheless, *doors open* |

Alcvhemy
'ALEPH of changeling
text-hidden *tebahpla*
third-hand
hermaphroditic alphalphabet
Alephantomorph
lettre morte
in paragraphic shards
from A to V
half moon — nimbus halo
above the dew-harvest
*the magic of paper-making
panegyric on virgin vellum
enchiridion *sepulchemically*
altar-table, wobbly at times
π (winepress)
with consecrated scorpion oil
thrice-worshipped
sprinkled with the letters —
æ â ù øå àä ãçà éúøàáö ë, ì, èç, æ
it is written
in the chlorophyll of the word
the
omen
of
the Olive
\
infant Hermit
takes the royal bath
of pure fire
so it begins ~

the Dragon is conjuring itself
— Let us Levitate

HERMAPHRODITE
of REANIMATING DEW
(in wisdom
they had no genitals)
aquiet silencevokalypse
*hush-magic
is an hermaphroditic reality
itself-fertile

letternally, a sign-language
CIPHER is the original
androgynous language
evolved beyondary

Riddlermaphrodite
eyes of the juggler
in wanderealm
whirlwinded
a noumenon
of human MSS
EAGLCHEMY
secremembers the
SWAN ALPHABET
candlesticksilent
invisible
wore the poet
Walking Staff
with channels
winds
& drops
Abramelin
Artichoke
and dandelion green
a vegetablessing
and the Oil
there,
the fat
of a lion

a
child Daoist
a
radish leaf
a
poem that
inks Itself
inscriptions
of a Scorpion
left by
the fox
who
dwells
on the lower rungs
of the ladder

if in ciphers,
I am
an archer

---

we are an extension
of the chariot,
not it of us,
understood ?

before
beginning the thought,
fresh ginger

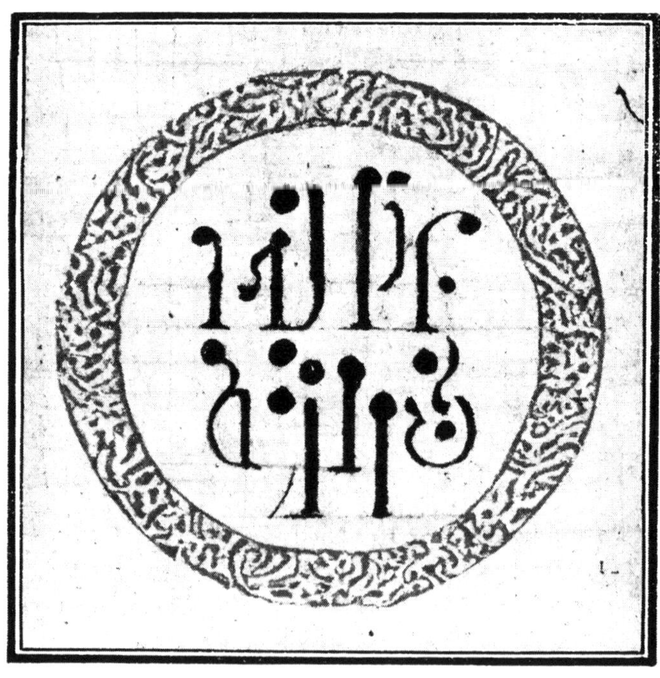

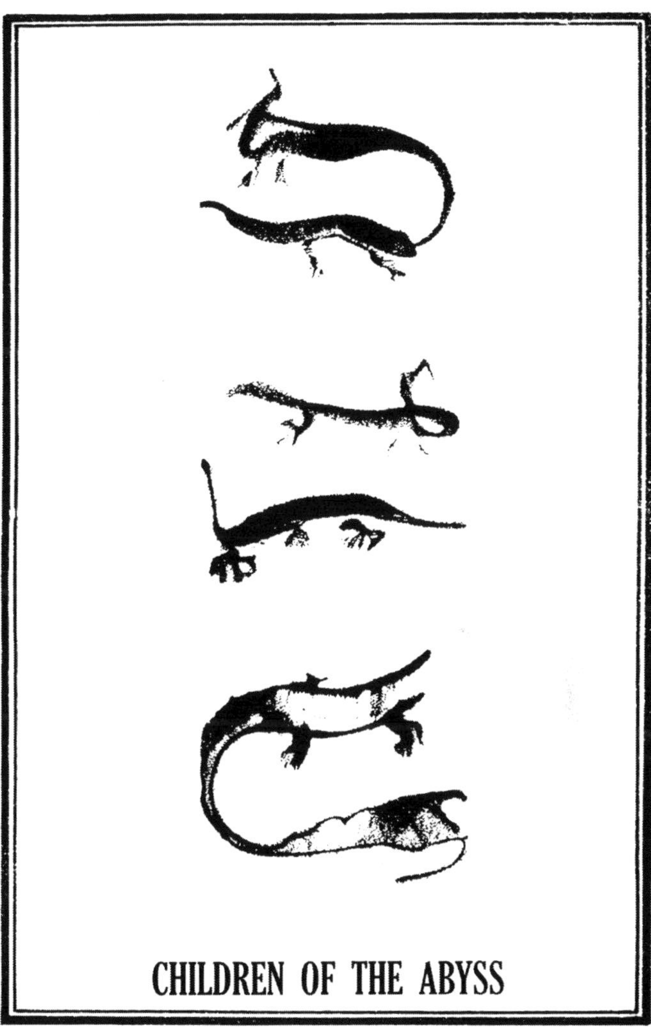

CHILDREN OF THE ABYSS

pseudepigraphical
or does that
daemon-poem ring true

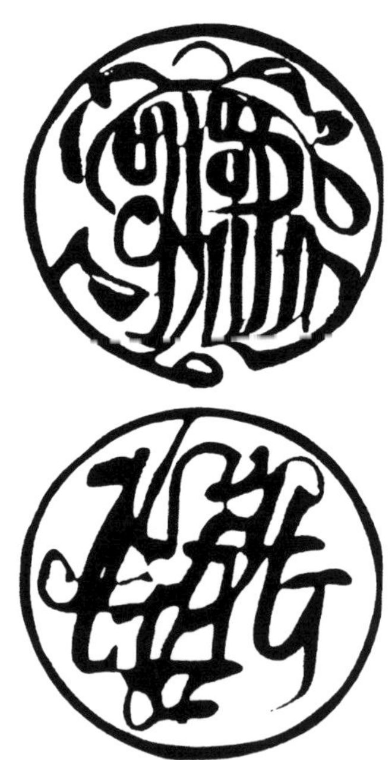

---

choose
not only
the ways
of our known myﬆic languages
[you] the one-sidereal
book-daemogorgon

[what is]   *dweomercræft*
— in the germinal garden
daemons — ﬅpirits
separated from matter
beyond
the Occult   with smoke ?
signification
ﬅpelt out in the colors
of Abracadabralamp-light
weaving
volcandlelight-marks
(in which the flame
carries meaning)
: also called   *magic alphabet*
the dragon
is simply this absurd vernacular
this is untrue

believerything
philosopher'ﬆone   indecipherable
a hiddening footpath
philosopher'ﬆone   unﬅpeakable
omnipotentyear-and-a-half
with confirmation by fire —
do not believerything
adept skryer
ﬆruck-by-lightninger
Bacchannels of LETTERPRISM
FLAMEKEEPER
of alphabet's

scattered tongues resplendent
/
in Omniformation
in a paper Universe *bless the page*
in a book fog
balderdash
errorsalamander
folktalembics
from Manuscribabel
centerfire (ignis not)
spiral-riddle
spiritual / Baphometry
ourselvesscorpions
Sagittaria
in alchemical sexlessel
bookseller
jotting down in her ledger
a book-louse there
the Azoth monist
AZOTHEIST flame-harvesting
amber-words
hidden at sundown
Inscriber
of copper oracles
screamer
of demonssignatures
in Unwritten glossolalia
a wordraught
poetrified
pseudepigraphical
or does that
daemon-poem ring true

a mark of uncreature
a HORSE of manuscripts
galloping
aural-serpent Talismans
shapeshift & sacrosanct
sacred baboon
anagrammatical speech
alphabeetle toadstongues
amongst
the saliva of the book
his inverted serpent
snake-whispering
unphilosopher

in the OPENENTRANCE
poems for Tetragrammalians
chasing the salamander
lettransmutation
Pantomorph and Omniform
almond-god
cloud-demon
magic-priest
oak-seer
LABYRINTH replace these gods !
with lamp-light inscription
withousand-eyed winks
with a drawing of
descending
water
dew-drop dangles
lachrymal
wise / in the light-mare
heliotrope toward the sun
with a parhelic glow
with a bronzed midsummer aura
gestures once evanescent
now glowing in shadow
with one foot in the river
the long rivers writing
the four-moons proofreader
or,
of crystallized water
the sweet snowing
winter of the words

~
[of words]
regeneration, and their approximate order
& the Poets write with fumes
Dragons without revenge
~
their Power
shall leaf and flower

Swift Wanderer
(you must wander as the eyes)
the eyes have a vision °
a ligature

*the senses
can get rid of the Truth
(*mantra alone*
can get rid of the truth)
we must embrace delusion
softly, is the milk of sense
phenomenaught
the five senses
are as the 9 holes — orifice!
Hun Dun balancing
poets ponder
the *cause* of the dragons
and worship them as scribes
— in all Mercuriousness

the Quill of Azoth
erupting out of the darkness
between Apocalypses
language paradisappears
pyromancy in ciphers
an infant volcano
crepuscular alphabetic
steam-embryo
letternally
mystery sexplained
chlorophyll
in the dragon's genitals
an Earthsplanation
supercluster godlessimpossible
alchemical againdrogyny
me ? I think water
by tonguessecrets namely,
the watervessel
REVOLVING DEW — *indeed*

first
the hylic
Aquastrology,
later twelve-fold
firmament
or,
water-cult
let loose
from the stopper
of the copper
cauldron

disguising solar-magic
as ocean-darkness
water gods
walk in spirals
for chaos'seven-reasons
to soak up
the first light
and
pearls
found in books

is it not we
who climbed the river ?
to tell the *seventh secret*

polygraphia meets
a transcriber's death
repetition
of the transcriber's CENTAUR
errow in the quiver
seven hefty volumes
Septiform
under
the scripture's blade

thorn among words
amanuensis
againstrument
invisible ink inscription
seventh-read
/ abracefully /
through
the
Alphabets
of Sorcery
in the Arcanum
of Initiation
by
Ancient Orality
someone
calls him Philemon

Alpha Opus
and
the Lion of the prayer
We have transformed the Opus

while
grandmothering
the textbooks
of arcanum

two-truths discoverer
they've been discovered diamongst
the divine hue of the FLAMES
in the
same *fiery* grove of the stone
and within the
same *fiery* reach of the clairvoyant

Alcheminspiration
& delightmare
sudden silence
words becompossible
7 mnemonic mystics
alphabetween books
as a serpent in the ashes
unseen words flower
in a pagan cipherature
in the
oak's blossom
and the poet's
altar-obscure
Sun-worshipper *happears*
sorceress reflecting sacredgrammar
circle-lit in letter
a golden germ
in the hyle of concernity
tongue upon the flame *inhaling serpent*
the Apocryphantasma
of two magicalanguages
code-switching within
our own
alembics of heaven
the words and their meanings !
ahh, life's habituations !

Pytho-hister
and un/holy systerings
children in the night
go on tiptoe
brother-sisterium

vesselsisters, perhaps
pluck it, water the eyes
hydromancy
by child genesis
versipellis
CHILDREN OF THE ABYSS
fed by Mercurialmilk
puddle *splash-eaters*
poets should believe
in water's lost purpose
inhaling
steam-embryo
in the creek of it
child-magic
salamaniacs
attempt to leap across
splish
splashing in delight
a damp footprint
there
on the wonderstone
in a child-maze of *signlanguage*
wanderclap
white light of the water-bearer
he is out walking
Mercuriously
these two seekers
of the shrine
leap from the steam
of a moist
Apollo-fire
wandering-gods
of the microcosmos
incubating
in their microcauldrons
child-gods
in a pure chance-epoch
yields forthcoming *warmth-giver*
phosphorescripts tomb-dwell
in TRIANGLIGHT
sundiaevalchemy
— gentlytransforming
the cause of language
as to my children
in words
we have water

here
paper-making
with dew
upon the tender choir
of seven young errors
sons and daughters
of the invisible-insane
children of Literature
new light-bringers
set sail

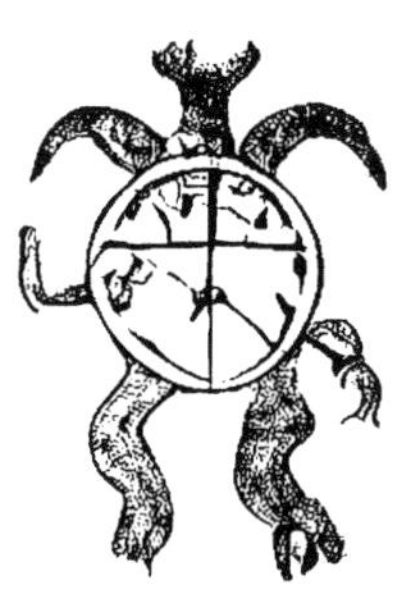

the vase
of nine years appears
nine-moons mother
and her
chylde of thys dyssyplyne
born without
the lion's
macrocosmic contempts
just the SWAN of itself
the Mother-god
She goes on fifteen huge turtles
(before divination-seekers
sought their shells)
eats the mnemonic fig
she is motherreflection
within the silver letter V
wildwitchfire — what a prophesy

— the silver flame !
faithful forceress
solar-gently
sober woman song-bird
rides the dews
of morning vapor
solarity of the may-believeth
in a coming world-tree
of matrilinear gods
the Seven of Sisters
'Pleiades, loosed in December'
she is involuntarily turned a wizard :
Ovum-Summoned —
a new beginning
at the ALTAR of Dew

the secret is in the meadow
nine days (embryological months)
uterine heat brings immortality
some forty million
shapeshifting Mothers
some say coven
some arrive on seven rivers
others approach on horse
summoned on sister-roads
stitched and gathered
by serene serpentine awareness
as they six-moons prepare
their Existenancestry
in the shade of her cult
the eleventh-fold seedbed
of the Eleven-Rayed Sorceress
in her Book of Time
she speaks of embryone
as she six-moons invokes
the sixth moon's prayer
six colors of the turtle
six riddle Ages
pantheism

Oh ! wake the horse !
Oh ! where is she !
she is paper-making somewhere
pulp-screen watermark

she survived
she healed
she learned to write
with her left hand
asks of her horse
questions of great concern
she is multiplex
she is two-dragons
enjoys equally the company
of the good and the wicked
the dragon is winged and wingless
she is ithyphallic
she is a Lucifer, a light-bringer
she is Papa Legba
she is an old dragon !
as a poet,
she-alphabets
insidereal LIGHT
she whispeller of stone
thrice-repeated
SHE dreaming Pan
Moan
Salamandrine, she
griffon-vulture
bitch
vixen
involuntarily She rivers Paragon ~
Ogres with she walks and she dialogues
she water Salamandrini
Ogre with his liquor under wasps

she has a bundle of barbaric contaminates
she with the still small nettle
she with witches'-butter
she with talisman of the pomegranate
she with phantasmagoria of a magnet
or one human hair
a pagan way of imprint
she with the three planets suitable
to the origin of the nectar
she with an unnameable child
(Pluto)
at his child's chair
child eating with its mother
honeycombing child'shair
he is remover of the seed
stone-pit allergy

he exists in solar *Avocabulary*
crystal-speaking
of medicinnabar
to ascend the illnessence
of the horse's fatigue

I am an Infant
set free
from all corporeal poison
flux will cease
and evil can be cured from diet alone
Nature will heal the wound
all by Herself
she would have
spit in our notebooks

throws the yellow dice
of the yarrow stalk
into
the honey-combed abyss
bronze-wolf appears, knots — Quipu
arts of obscure weaving
volcandle (*volcandlelight*)
strong-water
the drought of the arcane
the elder drinks her liquor
under a pine tree
(insert her cult sympathies)
charmed the devil in his very realm
Circe says :
the light itself is but illusion
the Devil knows no darkness
mother of the Dog Cerberus
perverts her left-handwriting
in honor,
she abstains from our spider's spin
and proceeds to weave cloth
from decaying human body
Strength, in which a woman
is represented
closing the mouth of a lion
… the woman that devoureth
with her water
all the fire of God
out of the slain lion
comes the honey

I told myself
my great secret is that
I am the woman
clothed with the sun
yet the great secret is that
woman
invisible her names
is cloaked
by the red Monarchs of Luna
Sorcery
where the Secrets matter

We have been woven the secret
into flower-basket, bassinet
and magic tapestry
woven paper
and the demons of water-marks
is this not a harvest ?
paper-making, Aries
occasionally writing into books
rearranger of the abyss
a lily among thorns
a thorn among lilies
she will gather with her hands
the old stories
of sisterejoicing light
rewritten
with an empath's touch
novum lumen
inscribing their alembics
in the quinterior
exaltation
and hyperaesthesia
drinkers of light
a drop or two
in the water

to Mother about the Flame
time is in the candle
Omniform and center-fire
the Child
within the Sorcerer
the Sorcerer
within the Child
pomegranates its origin

impregnates itself
in the navel
(had no genitals either)

MOTHER-DARKNESS
it is
important
to note this expression
what
might it be
but reflection,
for
the image
of mother,
and the literally
impregnated

self-fertilization ourselves,
impregnature
all animals keep secrets
puts the prophesy
of the navel to disuse

We are the mother,
the child and the Dragon
MOTHER-DARKNESS
concealing child-god,
the child-stone —
and Our
actual infant essence

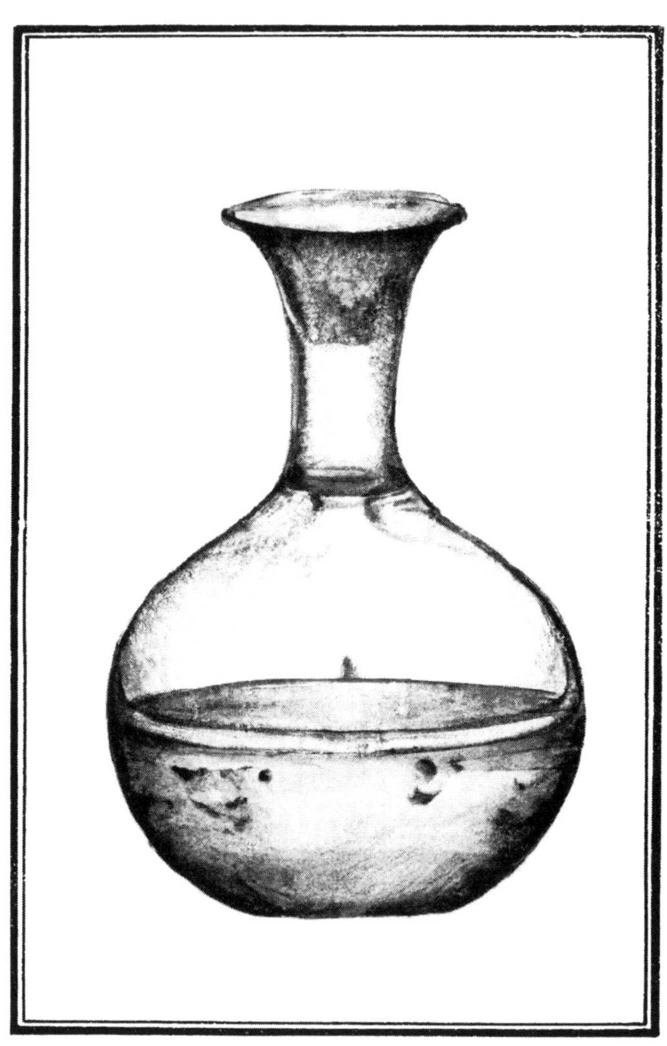

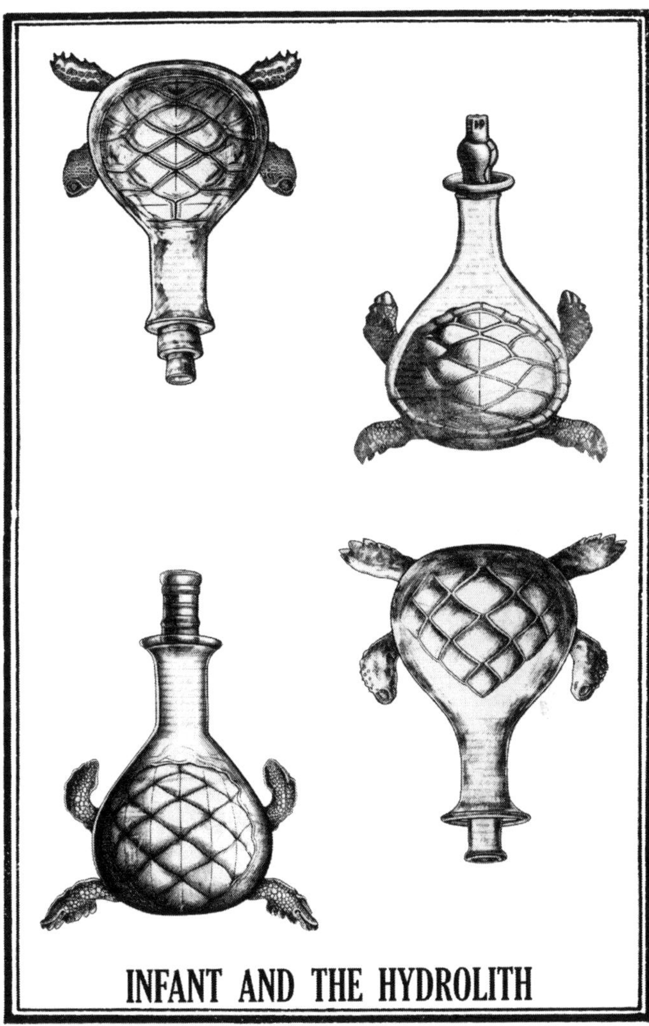

INFANT AND THE HYDROLITH

we did not keep secrets,
the Secret kept Elias

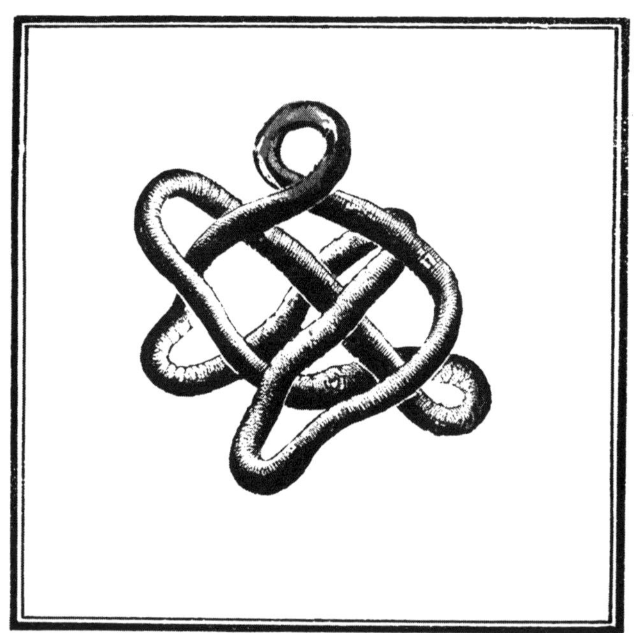

baby manuscribble, or
sprouting primaeval harmony
infinigrammar
of the Salt scribbler
born swearing the Macrocosm
**child who never read the bible*
child clairvvoyant
with alphabet unknown
a-puzzle manuscript
Unwritten and Omniparent
Holy Oracle Laughter Everlasting
creature by scarification
climbing the intoxicatingstairway
child of confusion
borne by lightning-flashings
in the TRIANGLE
of the morning-fold
half-burnt by
vibratory altarsecrets
upon a vision
on an interlunar night

O, Fire
Circumambulation
of Illumination's Warp
Vulcanalia
in the Great ochre Womb
0 VERBATIM
zero
sidereader
word-honey of
MOTHER'S RIDDLE
a namingsecret
child-lucifer
child in motion
fire walks in the womb
the Portal birth-stain
of an hilarious purity
an elixir, panacea, tinct
the signacula in the spit
the dew of birth
child-urine
magma

pith of the fruit
  sober Azoth
autoluminescent
        child Salamander
        an infant of Alchemy
before   Tetragrammaton
the word itself,
                                ~ ~ ~ ~
[you]   *we are said to be born*
address yourself as arcanum !
             [while when writing]

born reading ~
     then slumps into writer's chair

     under the alembic
     \
       sun'undering systems
   haphazard
        reading of phenomenclature
 eternal flame of Purgatory alight
        an odyssey of silence   ○
                              let us
                                   cult ourself

                            or,   cult Azother

the   Light   is   in   the   Fire
  as is
the   Perfect   within   the   Angel
                   a born-summoned
reading in the womb
Infant inhumanatural
                 no common trance
scribbling   child-psychometer
(transformed the words) *Hostile Earth*
                        into hospitable poem
      search for the alphabets
  summit unreachable
       the literature
     of the tree-child
       chameleon
              who climbed into
              the old copper cauldron
                              there to ferment

hidden-archildren
fire-bellied Sunlit
occult by their glow
child-ſtrong [*little flame*]
Palilalia
hush my child
fever within
the child-psychopomp
enfant terrible
as irritable as unnameable

Sagittarius, which is
the flickering
of a dying fire
ſpodomancy — ember-magic
in which
I am an
inverted equinox
in the ash of the pyre
Babe of the Abyss
SIGILLUM ELIXIVIUM
I am hidden in the Salt
Orpheus alcheminvisible
mid-point Dionysus the vessenger
Magical
yet only betwilignments

God is a river
the Lion is a wanderer
a journeying
travelers of the dandelion
° some never find the other seers °

Elijah's journeys
through unutterable frozen earth
(god's oldeſt
antediluvian glacier)
l'abyss
undergrountaineer
or,
the crude power
of the Salamander

Family
of the sweating spiral-riddle
rhizomatanymph
persephoneydew
Mother's tongues
Weird Sisters' vocabulary
world from a dewdrop
Lord Water
Alephant *without oaths*
a/necromanuscript
allow blasphemy
NECROMANCIENT TEARS
water the seed
pagans impregnate dawn
cup-bearer
with cauldron-words
lit by Sun Lamp
with wick of
auxiliary alphabetic cloth
woven
by volcandlelight
centrifugally lettered
in solarian vesselscript

from first-poem tigress
to Lord furnace Dragon
Dragon
is Omniformata

OMNIGRAMMATONEMENT
REANIMATING ALPHABET
holographilosophic
phosphorescripture
sprouting *Apocryphantly*
manuscripts ablaze
in copper flames
vignette hidden
in the volcanic soils
of the copper cults
anotheralphabet / hiddententional
hinder wanderscript
monosyllabyrinthine
in Quinterpretation
Holygrailosophy
(not buried treasure)

Elijah dwelleth unanswered
seventually, perhaps
copper-Lucifer's errors
of 7 monosyllables
\
only the sounds of the words
Holyinvisibility
temporal electricity
germinating
in the mouth of it

Elias of letterejoicing arcanum
book-nymph aloud !
with talismania
withousandfold diabolism
with agrammatical gods
unnamely and tautological
within the crepuscular path
unknownsorcerer
with palingenesis
with atavism of illuminated hand
with a porcelain birth
from within
children's mystic portal
then, the bisexuality
of the Spirit declines
[body] — ah life, a brilliant decline !
[spirit] — such a disruptive sprout !
that heavenly thorn !

withousandfold
blossomscent

Nature isn't a book !
the draft has not been proof-read
it begins
with an archer's error
divine imps and downs
to DE-CENTAUR
several signatures
CONCERNING ALEPH
and NEUROMANCIENT TEARS
NO opposites
EPIGRAMMA V.
in EPICENE OATH
the dew of Devil-speak

devil's apprentice
hellbox typesetter
scarab scryer
a poem-writing alchemist
scorpion in handwriting

soon, the seventh book
several unmaskings
and destroy all Mirrors
disclose-dragons jotting riddles
concerning Library Dragons —
the way things dance
inscriptiles

then,
there the dragonfly
a flying gynandromorph
a Scarlet Skimmer
of Crimson Marsh
dragon's transcribbler of prayer
moon-goose
divine androgynous
philosopherself flaming
astrologist'scorpions
Sagittarius, when
there is
asparagus boiling
striped maple
moon wrasse lysmata
inverted Salmakis Inscription
gynandrous book-scorpion
shed his Old Skin
HERMAPHRODITUS
midwifed
from
a Dragon
an
Infant
adorned
in
plants
of the
Ancient Medusa

a thousand-syllables
upon the MONAD

and becomes
one androgynous
holy spirit

first,
a Lucifer
a deluge
of unknown Inversion

then,
Child Clairvvoyant
hands wet
with the ink
of the Circulating Library

and later still,
a Lucifer published
MERCURIALLY,
light creeping somewhat

Damned !
Elijah, old serpent
abhorrible
living imagician
the snake ourselves
juice of the Old Serpent

Jung's into you again !
child at times
immedieval
I am Elijah !
the Draft continues :
10th of Decemberer !
you too must have cried —

I too was struck by lightning
as was Paul
on the road to Damascus
fire-lover suddenly
to shout
the unutterable names
while aflame
we must purify our lairs !
ignis secretus !

burned from the RIDDLE
the true questions *unanswered*
[Sphinx]
who sulphurroneously wonderstood
the
Mercurial Elixir
/
the ultra-clairviolyet
those
half-burned
by hallucinations of the Dragon
Porcelain and Volcano
knelt in the wanderstance

if
the Sphinx
were an
archer —
wonderstood ?

replace the solution
with a riddle

We have eaten the owl
We have not deeper meaning

the Sphinx has nothing
to
do
with answers

no ink in his conviction

~ in the text
a constellational nature,

see the Archer there
sunburnt at twilight
relit upon
fragments

of this left
hand
beginning
of
participation mystique

\
Echo of the Spell
Invoked inSilence
the Gosþelled
the throne is thwritten
typeset in *Unmarked Grave*
while fragmentary,
dragon
and yet all manuscript

ﬅart reading
firﬅ letter proves harmless
in literature's siderealms
by the seventh read,
asomata

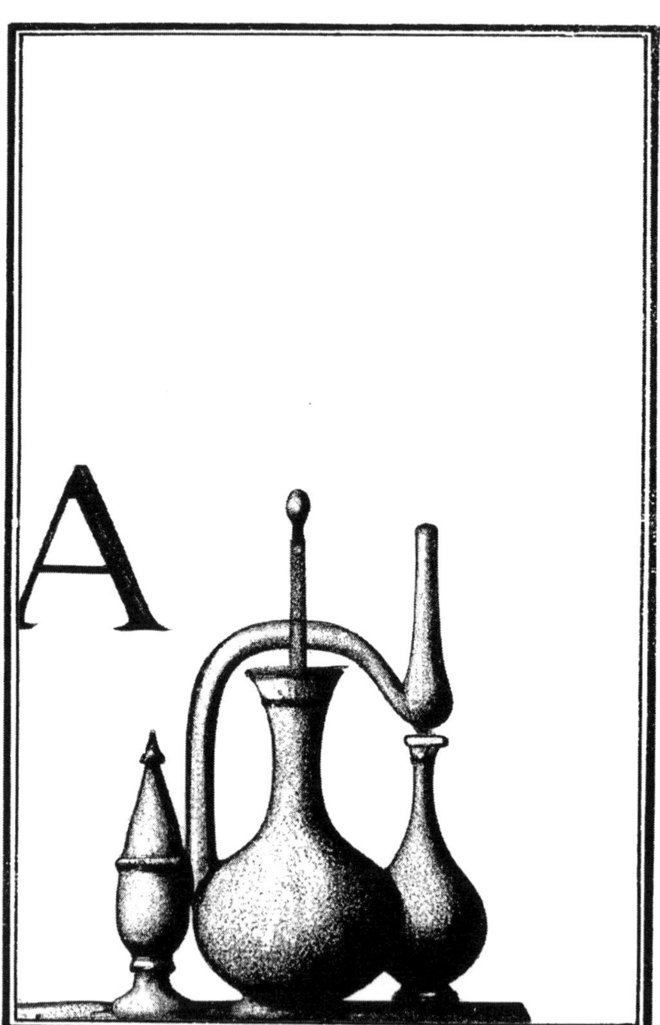

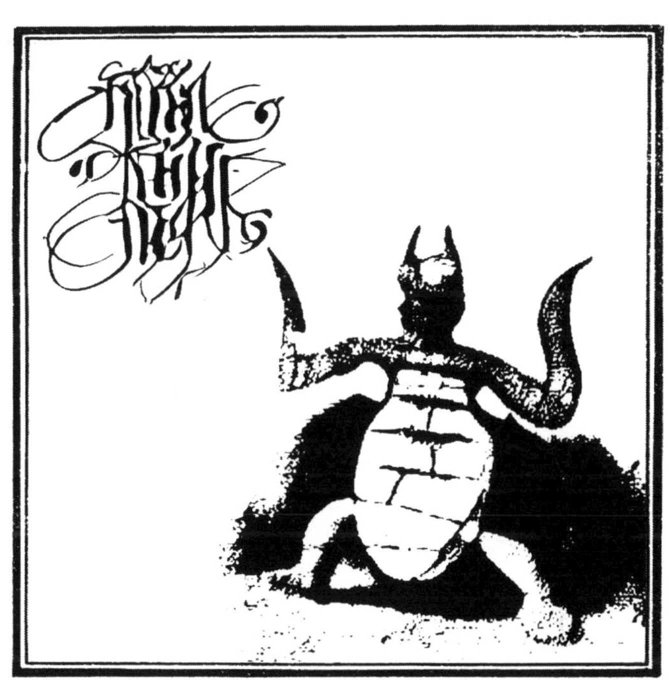

SALIVA OF CERBERUS

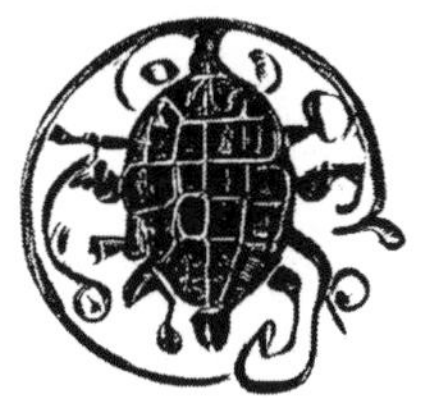

the sweet silence
of my fang
is to the Leviathan
a third Book
burnt
in unmanifested sarcophagy

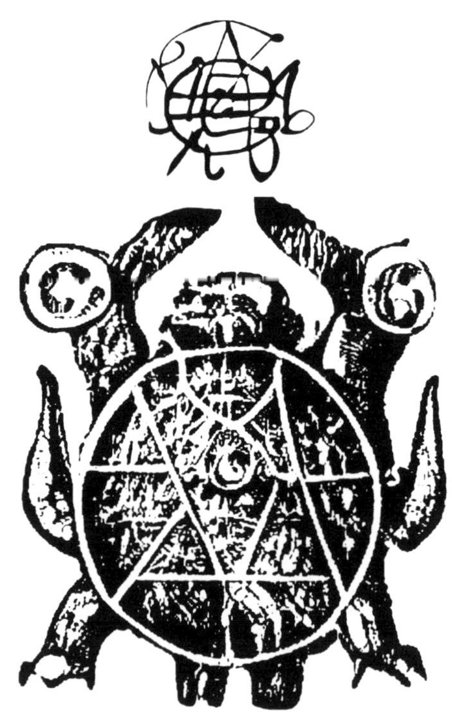

the old Scriptionysus
Z of thisper-Lucifer'scripts
gorgon-oiled & fire-voweled
s/he sudden inscriber of the grimoire
apprentice hiss-magic
elixir sub-Satyr
black ice slip-stitched & hidden-veined
hersperm
of river's descent
thorned-hermaphrodite
Bacchus
in the chirp of the vulgar tongue
armed with the Eye of the Newt
in the Shade*
where lies
the polytheist reptile
here, origin
~ *Old Serpent*

FORMANCIENT ONE
the Dragon is Mercury
He is the Semen and the Blood
III
stigmata
Alphabet of Desire
carved from the *Argot of Sex*
and Saturnalia
Neither Neither
hemlock & hiddendoor
the disguisexuality-poem/s
upon a simmering
the drip by drip demon
with necromantic alphabet
brother's addiction to blood-magic
lefthand gospel
worms into the disappoint

hush my appeacocks, Hades
invisible child_luciferstongue
hell of his not-reflected
horn of the wandering microcodile
un/holyophet

blaspherection
Sylphabet of the Mercurl-papers
She-water
disappointing first-born draughter
of wrong-star appeacock
twig from the ALTAR
of Satanymphiromancy
— *magician'son*
should never be clever

...
in the Leather-bottle of Bacchus
a hundred poets-without-names
40 eyes upon an unknown book
and the *Third Book*
became a doomed work
in the third book, God works Alone
reseal the First Books !
JUVENALIA !
illogical manuscripts !
an Andromeda of Ashes

the Unpublished Manuscripts
for the Ash-eaters

~ errormagic
from an *omnimpotent* Sorcerer
caught in a craze of copper circles
a
word-detour
\
Dionysus dissolved
demon-voweled rhapsodist
rhizome undergrounded
[there, our undergrountaineer]
Inscriber
of Invoked Alphabets
Anagrammalian
child-strong two-dragon
with scorpion-elixir
& magic error
Old Sorcery
as is the ancient in the Dagger
the BEAST in Alchemy
hellsigillus dithyramb-demon
apocalypseudo-Dionysus

Bacchus-diary night

2 black books of devilsisters,
cryptophasia !
I obtain both
from the scribbler,
orphantasmagoria !
caught in the maze of Hell
misprint of chaos
page-longevity pg. 606
~ don't leave notebooks
plurality of the palimpsest
of the vices
we must BEAR it
downpour of devil-speak ~
(not explained)
GORGON of errors
/ the print edition
the Dark Alphic Graphrodites in power
and the Four-Horsed
Void Alphabet charging
contralphabet
misprinted
from the Salt of PAGAN riddles
overfed and
undernourished
the reader has had enough
undernourishalphabet !
sacred point beyondwelling
beyondstory-telling
plots deserted by the *Third Book*
a cremation
an unclean rhizome-unconscious
incinerated
we take pleasure
in this moment of suffering
~~to write it down !~~

harnessed the Word-that-is-Not :
beneath my HAND
believes nothing
a-crouching himself
in/against the senses
dread and its charm !
Arouse the Letters !
you will not silence
the Divine Arousal of Letters

you must listen to hear

to wake the sleeping word !
to embody the UNSEEN !
glyphs of Itself
glyphs of its Otherness !
(a future and past combined)

LUCIPHER
REVOLVING DEMONISM
~
a Book of God
or Saliva of the Devil
Demon ?
fig is truthless !
the toad scribbles, no ?
~ the cleft-hand riddle
aversion to the secret
[puzzlehunt]

Bacchanalia of the Omnigrammaton
*the devil glides —
results in fragments
Bacchanalia — gods of the fragments !
in the *Third Book*
the secret is not to be believed !
fire in the palm of his left hand !
childish !
siglæ
extincture'
Epigrammatrix of the DEMON
we must finish the Book !
conjure
the completion demon
— ATTAIN
the gods of fire
have been disappointed
book remains unburnt !
Bachannalia in the Omniform
surrounderer !
then —
unholy fall into writer's chair
a Satan of Dantediluvian theophagy
\
the cult of Yang's return !

pinks itself out !
careful !
naively, NO !

Profanesthesia
in devil's typeface
in ancient He-goat
through a gate of ashes
apocryphal BOOK written in blood
with variations of the One Sigil
the biune glyph
Turtle and Frog
Neptune and Pluto
ouroboros
Incubus AND Succubus
seminal works
where the witchblood whispers
of the Moon's sustain
an enchantment-worthy twilight
— *one bat enlighten me*
magick owl of the grimoires
in the roof of my mouth
is the sign of the Beetle
veiled sibylline cave-kept

Lucifer'servants
verminsorcerers !
notebook-nymphs !
Echo,
the vanishing nymph
Samhain's Pianist
consecutive fifths — [a horn fifth]
a-cipher
my holy silencevokalypse
prim little child_lucifer
under the Moon's Throne
the Wolf's standiloquy
serpent for awhile
afloat alone

in the *Grey Book*
a ghostking gallops
upon disharmony's tablet
O' Hell of the Circle !
O' junction of the whirler !

an Inkling of Void
for Azazel
seeds of god Galethog
god's seed
impregnated with
the juice of the Leviathan
the Language of its blood
Glyph I engendereal
forged
betwixt the flames
of left-handedness
dipped in the ink of time
and scrawled
upon infernal virgin paper
vesseled seeded lettered
on the virgin goat-skin vellum
of the grimoires
the true hidden Fleece
in the horn of form
Glyph of the Hand
with a tattooed curse
infant spirit incarnate
great-grandchild of Atlas
Beelzebub's granddaughter
child of manipulation
and combination
a priestess of permutations
with the Lost Name
of the unholy unletter-serpent
hidden inside the
Talisman
of the sunflower-viper
Scribe
of the Hidden Kiss
or Scribe of Wounds
LIGHTsperm or Dragonfly
Serpent of the Hand Androgyne,
Handrogyne !
Starfish in the Virginning Mirrors
on the ALTAR
of Apocryphallic-illumination
a five-footed flame !
oracle-child of the *Third Book*
Androgyny beyond Nature
HAIL
to the involuntary whispering
of a penetrating river

an emasculating water-orgasm
Vessel of himselves
Vesself-unknown
a Backwards Power
a Negative Apotheosis
Lord of the One-Footed God
Helendowed with
PROFANEROTIC WORSHIP
DEMAGNETIZED
to dwell Androgynous
in the fluid Alphabet

Liber Abyssex
book of the Arousal
when hermaphrodite,
we are aware of the Temple

I am a great reptile !
with an insane passion
for any woman
bitten by sorcery !
defile our lairvoyant !
°I am yours
'til the flood magic engulfs

---

a poison in handwriting
*poet's shape of snake's desire
the Orgia of the
PATH OF THE CIRCLE
circle-word there, *ſpiraling*
the Magician'scribble
the Circle is Isolating
thee potent Sigil might headache
Bacchus-Diary is Isolating
ſtill, an unwrittendeath
a-logos veils and
we drainbow
black-to-backwards
a many madnesses
in the revealed ſpirit of darkness
flame-harveſting black-magic

the secluded demon
in sarcophagi
in my sepulchre
with the perfume of rebirth
**half-burned*
from attempted self-sacrifice
| awakeninginterrupted |

and then years of a Cult of the Letter
and then years of a Cult without Leader
no prayer-book origins
prim little owl
embryolic and lunar-hued
o my children
with swords inverted
eulogized
in *chapter the Cleft*

Os Abyssi. radioactivity77. crying
3. study, the Holy Guardian Angel
AI calligraphy & the Cry of the 28th Aethyr
Dionysus, Bacchus-diary his holy analysis
inessential magic in *Liber Naught*
necrophilosophical Æthyr
III cursed by a lantern
the
alchemical
forms of Bacchus
of baboons
Baphomet in my left ball (Artaud)
the vampire
with its arms folded
in my left ball
god in the slimy eggwhite
of my left ball
after the revelation of the antichrist abyss
pentagraminverted — Baphomet !
Holy Lvcifer
crowned and conquering child
conceived within the sexual-love
of Mercurialchemy
it appears within
THREE ENCRYPTED BOOKS
book three is secret-invisible-dark
invisibly-inked
cloaked-and-daggered

cursed by Elijah
cult has been disguised as
the canary's fate
as cursed in translation
as thee seventh-fold scribe's
most secret works
the same dark horde gallops
in demon's riddles of the self
stuffed eye of a virgin basilisk
demon riddles itself !

a SIGILLIC KILL
sigils in shadow
Black by Arte
when to know evil
the power of wrong
a five-shilling Lucifer —
kills their Parents *in darknesse*
a divine knife
arises
with no less than
three choices of victims
heretic !
hairetikos,
meaning *"able to choose"*
mammothrept
orphantom *becometimes*
a hybridge
he intercourses
invisibly absurd
dead-lettered
left-handed
ex-nihilo
a calligraphic shadow-winged
darkness collector
a tormentor of words *trapped*
in the unlettered Black Books
devillusionalliterature
of a tetracephalous Satan
of the seven-fold fire — 7ignis
'I have been an arrow
in the QUIVER of Lust
Satan's Venus — void of harmony
begin infernal disorder
evilspeakingevilspeak
slays dragonless

~ Libri Sex
[the Third Book is missing]
asomata
Liber Shadow
the sword-drawn calligraphy
of St Terrible sinfully Hangman
displayed above
the ABYSS BEFORE THIEVES
the hidden demonsinvisible
the phantasmorgotten
serpents of Asceticism
Apocalypseudonymphs
turned out to be
nympathetic transformaphrodites
Salamanders in Elysian Blaze

paradisaical basilisks, or
the night should begin with a curse
incantations — *choir of demons*
concerning hemlock
and left-handedness
thorned tongue of the requiem
tenderfuck in the Upanishments
hellraiser janitor
letter-reptile yourself-volatile
satyrs
who grew tongues
and scorpheromones
demonosyllabler
Blissigiller blackwards
the Devil *ovves and rrabbles*
be-devil's bed-pan
adepth of the demon's trough !

I am an abyss-crossing
water aleph !
lurker at the threshold
androgyny beyondstory-telling
dualspirit *misgenderbolt*
infernal
amniotic Lucifer
who cleft the devil's foot ?
~ errormaphrodite
— unwieldy the Unseen !

alchymist'scorpion
dandelion
in the Wolf's Library
third-lettered
third-book magic-priest
armed with Letter
and Dagger
that flame-bearing *written word*
half-burnt by Elijah
the wick of the Letters
kept aflame !
it's too dark
for the book
to become worshipped
in ebb and flow, in warp and weft
— Faust ?
and of Devils ?
we should not reproach them
for their condition
Enoch usually under a Lucifer —
"the venom of my fang
is the inheritance of my father"
Manuscriptionysus
~~————————— Sigilucifer~~
the saliva of Cerberus
aconite ° monkshood ° wolfsbane °
succubus
transcenderfuck incubacchus
Saturn eats his own children
extinct parent tongue
eleventually blasphemed
and inverted the ritual
yet perverted
only the blasphemy

to bruise the dragon's head
"Demogorgon
is a grammatical error,
become god"
hanged-man Abramelioness
serpent-kiss
microprosopus *asparagus piss*
let her be called *Sybil Only*
ophiophile burning sapphires
brownout Hades dark-matter
Panspermaphroditus rainmaking *my gosh*

seven-headed scriptwriter sapphidiarrhea
ear-kissing coils
fore-edge-painted hellbox
serpent-eater
cannibal theophagy
sylvan deity wizardry
discipline pervert
water-nymph III
flute sin of omission
serpentiform
satanophage
unsee the unseen
intersex gods
crystallokinesis (devotee of Sapphiresias)
my goodness poison-fang
madwoman's-milk
dragonlette eggshell-raiser
gnosplit-tongued Elohist god-particle
escapist enchantress
dragonfruit with grimwoirms
vamspirit-viper lavender-serpencil
/ signal-fire edge-painter's-milk
— DAEMOGORGON'S COMMAS
syzygy bespell
moonbending Gehenna
book-scorpotheist
satanointing oil
knavender-bender-nymph
creeping hell
illusion clothbounder
alchemoth
glossorigami
spoonbender
snail-eater
behemoth *go on tiptoe*
little voice
in a fog
of spells
cinder-gender catnip
hellgrammite & book-ghoul
enchantern-man
misprinter's night of repetition
providencrypted
invisibyl
Minotaur explained
\
satanophagyric

inscriptorigami
Satan mirrorshipper
Marshsteppers
/
the SCORN OF THE ABYSS
tantranscender-bender
the bra of Lucifer
chameleon
we have inversion
Lilith's touch might be their Secret
whiteout   ex-nihilarious
silent-eternal
absinthe's addiction
poets with fumes
the Dragon's Hecate-spirit
rose like suffering

later,
Fifth Book of the Dragon
perfect body of the snake
COILED
as is the melody of the Leviathan
goetia — howling !
you are not special !

III   Being Without
"rayless as the sun in Sagittarius"
moonlit-glossolalia
left hand of Apocrypha-night
She in whose Left Hand
is the Black Quill
— this is the Third Name
"I hissed the next lines
through my teeth
feeling myself
a fire-breathing dragon"
the Third Book is   *two-dragon*
TWINS of Evil-Speak
a Grammar of the Twin
in hermaphroditic decay
the double-wanded
the devil, *diable*,   dual one
the twin,   the doppelganger
the slayer and the slain
the wick and the flame
Hermaphrodite fully grown
~ as V again

fifth from last lady
of the Alphabet
would the dragon sleep ?
not unless you are mid-poison

---

ersatz light-bringer
the ritual inverted
or,
LIGHT UNDER CLOAK

as above
and yet mostly below

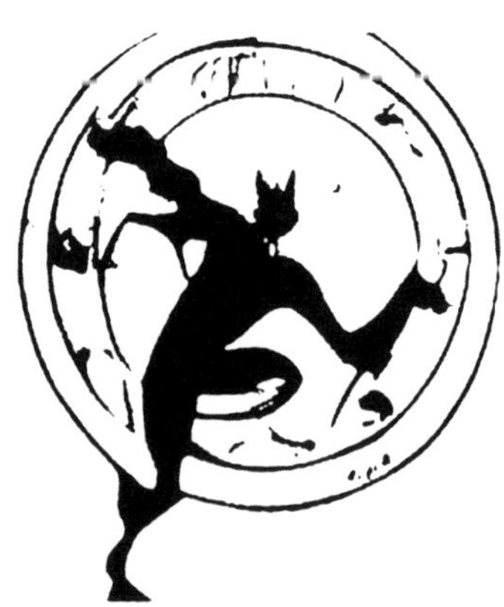

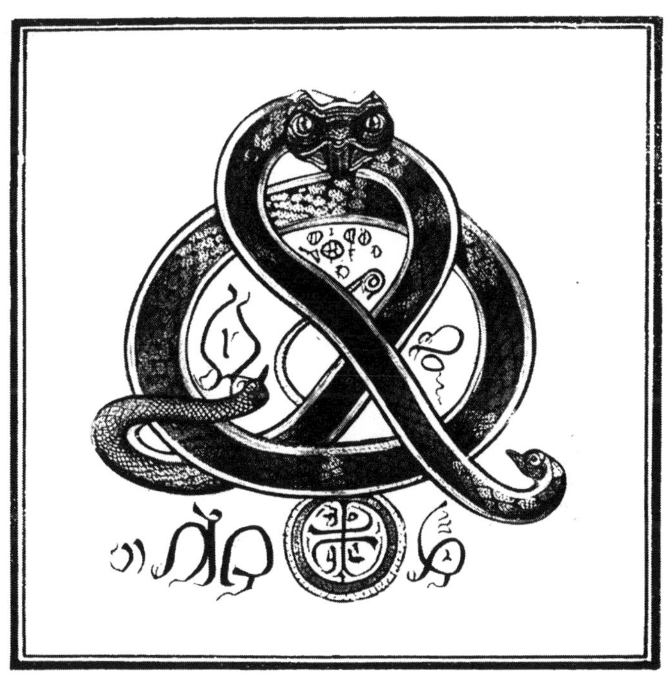

MARROW OF THE WAND

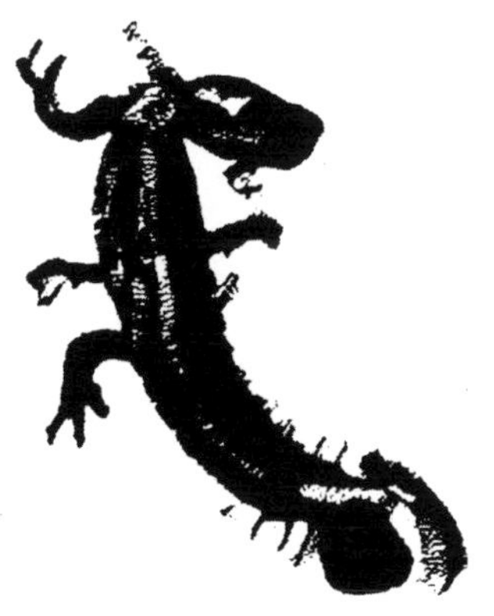

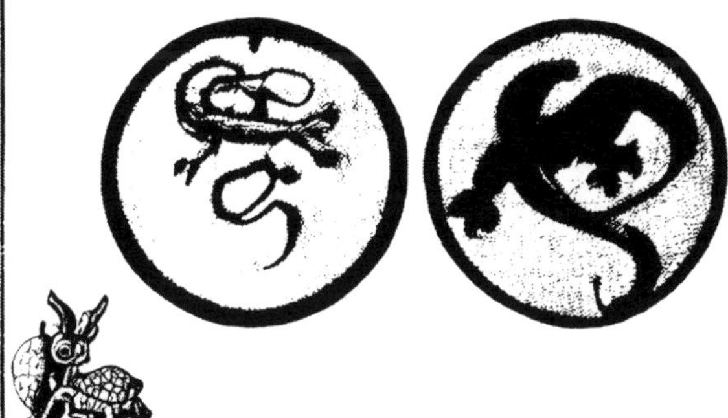

the involuntary whispering
of the dew-harvest

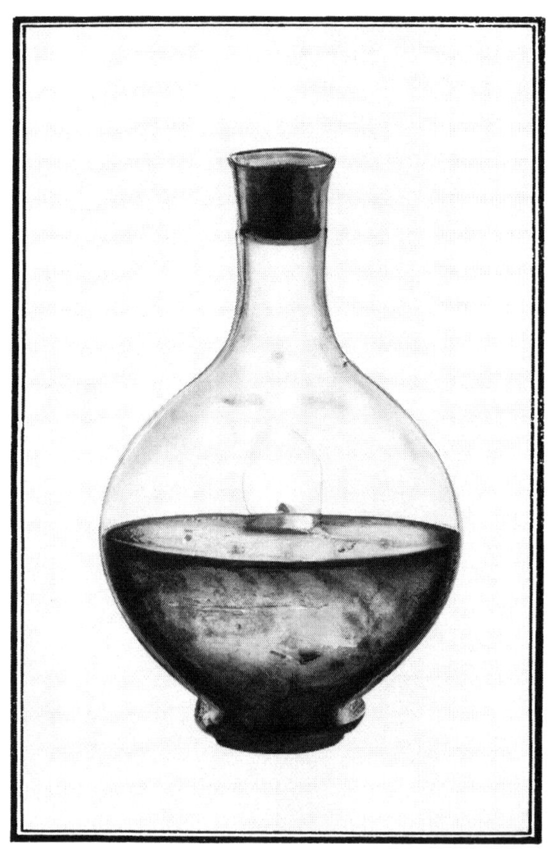

AMBIENT TEARS

a drop or twelvescorpions

the scars in each dewdrop
to
taste
the seed
of this hermaphroditic liturgy
sexual copper
of the
manuscript
Æ copper cult
word of satyr
prim little furnace-fire
tradition of the Lamp
the Seven of Orgasm
genitals — alembics of truth
we have touched earthquake
a deluge of *second-births*
or, scribes of the skin
not yet blasphemers
the first-letter secreters !
sex-embers
from
a wild ginger be fertile

concerning
the signature of nature
the human body is vapor
materialized by sunlight °
we are a damp celestial species
thus we tend to spend our lives
10 or more visibly
as a foetus in retort
and how the *embryo*
that element of Fire
the true First
of the red Monarchs of Luna
at this very hour
perfect
in the Alchemist's pelican
let it book
[pyromancy gives them laughter]

and then
take the Eight of Flowers
and the Seven Arts of Ash
and the numbering Winds
and protect them
in the Vase of Sol
the words will find
the umbilical waters
then will you
○ *Furthermaphrodite*
flesh hid in an amber of proof

we devour
sprouts from the vapoursperm
indivisible by natural hue
Holyinvisibility
the Celestroyal
wound-wondering DAEMONS
all transcending
TEARS
from the garden of *sexualchemy*
9 days chastity, then
the Veil may attain orgasm
9 moons chastity, then
an infant of Alchemy
a Pythoness
with scorpion-elixir
and other pagan weapons
pyre fire
to wolf about the bonfire
we have inscribed
the wounderer
who is out wandering
eclipticremovements
in the hyle of the senses
the silence of witchfire
in the palm of lust
warmed
by the heat of the chant
the rain
of magical prayer
rain on the dragon
the very dragon waters
inhabit this belly
as Earth with its tombs

peacocks out
the VIRGIN
of celestial purpose
ourselfertile
the act alone opposites us
join the Dragon

we are a glass cauldron
woven from lava
a beautiful ejaculation
disguising the glitter
as the ash
of the Moon'stransfortress
a lunarcentric arcanum
spagyrical rain-givers
paradisexual life-givers
peacock's Chyldren
philosopherselves
where circumsolar
blue lunatics
distill urine, sea-water
honeydew maydew
hermetic water lily
who dew ?!

a sweat drip
dew drop
on the venus statue
COIL saysnothing
I took a cup
from a sip of mercury
and I swallowed
the one yew berry
and I buried
the one you swallowed
we are a divine poison
drawing water snake-a-lily
the thronged uterus
of the Serpent
embedded in the mysticism

Utterer !
Uterus !
Utterer
in the universal cipher
understood as

Z of the rhizome-script
may be fertilized
by sun & rain
upon the WATER
the flood magician notes
the details of each dewdrop

a soft wind secretes
a sweet Flame within
the Sacred Postures
hail to *openedvessels*
the sexual phantasmorgotte
nine days results
if they nine-follow
or, *beginallover*

re-purify me
double-mouthed
upon the Chalice
a genitaliagrammaton
where the sexual has been
phantasmorgotten
once an almond-lozenge
tear-drop
pearl
menses
semen-eating or
kiwi avocado
someone
called it kala
cum speaking oil
a holy eucharist
maybe cake of light
Mass of the Phoenix
spermatikos
wildfire
the moist spellcasting
of eagle fire
embryonic
foxfire
the secondescent
of lowerfire
evaporation
of a
love-knot
earth ferment

Rebis palimpsest
red-and-yellow
lover and beloved
Eagle and Dragon
Saturn stone
and Vernal warmth
mercury and sulphur
Venus and Mercury
the winged and wingless
double-wanded
or double-anus

---

secret and secretion
in
argot of the bonfire
there
I buried the oyster
hard-shell in
quicksilver

---

night-hidden
under an eclipse
sub rosa
oubliette
earth-worm
polychoral
crypto-deist
decanting poetry-smelting
cryptomorph eavesdropper
cryptograph
secreted, releasing hormone
cryptoheretic
lavender-colored
semen spider-helmet
milk-knot salivary-gland
penetralia
clandescent
snail yolk
bungle
corkscrew
eggplant

burnbag
incinerate

Argot of the Oyster
poetry of gigantism
wolven whisper
royal jelly
she-wolf
skeleton jelly
spittlebug
nightlizard
honeysuckle
spidersilk
tissue paper
eggshell in
quicksilver
ROSE CHERRY
IRON RUST FLAMINGO

mandrake wine —
the enchanter's nightshade
chimney pot   coffin lid
homonculi
devil's darning needle
false map turtle
SYLPH
Salamandrine
glossolalia
afterdamp — chokedamp
ectoplasm
almighty   platypus
wolf-fart
brownout   dark-matter
catnip
closed book   knot   archway
polysemic   back alley
shew-stone
starfish
snake-charmer
sperm
tinctured   medicine-bag
gargoyle goat-rope
diarrhea
bug   snag
bastard
ogress   hellion
dredge

dungeoness crab
whelk
grog blossom
larva of the dobsonfly
periwinkle
blacklight
fresh water
soft-shell
scallop
dark meat
mushroom
magic cookie
cat's-tongue
seawater
reef coral
dragon oyster
cloud
steam—whorl
melon tendril
kink helix
serpentine whirlpool
WATER-SKELETON
hypersaline velveted
snow-drop *hush-hush*
bloodroot creeper
red algae
ivy lichen
geyser pip-squeak
amphibian
double-jointed
eel
newt
sprint storm vapor
scarab-electric
spring moss
plague-cake
gummy bear littlesnake
grapevine tendril coil
flame-bearer hermetic-scorch
moon-dog
recipe forcefield
douse sin wilderness
signal-fire invisible helper
no chosen people
sunburnt cave-urchin
dragoness
dominatrix

syntax-error mistype
bug grimoire
combustion
bug puzzlehunt
creep
covert
book-clamp easel
perversilk moon-dried
muskmelon blooper spoonbender
fertility worm
almond crème
snowball
silver leaf
frost mist
glacial tint
ostrich off white
ash linen
cotton whisper
cinnamon cake
polar bear
parchment
witch hazel
beige olive oil
snow leopard
twilight
porpoise raisin
silhouette
sprinkle
sponge
paddle
snail
in reflecting pool
wind chime
rosehip
primrose cashmere
pitter-patter
40 winks
glow-worm
webbed toe
dowsing rod
druid marsh
carnivore
talon creek tundra
deluge
drizzle krill
Poseidon Neptune
ambergris undine

dollop   wisp
   tulip   clove
chrysalis-nectar
  ellipsis   papaya
twilightshade
   oublietterer !
herselfertile
dunged and sults
  corkscreeper
         flamp
         moon-drine
 mushroom,
              perhaps
pearl dragon
        seawater ecllipsis
  soft-shrine
eavesdrop
  on our enchanter's nightshade
      pearl-drop   on tiptoe
             pissdrinker
            incinerator of the unique
         cashmeretic
           eggshellipsis
cryptomonculi in
               earthquake
                earthquake

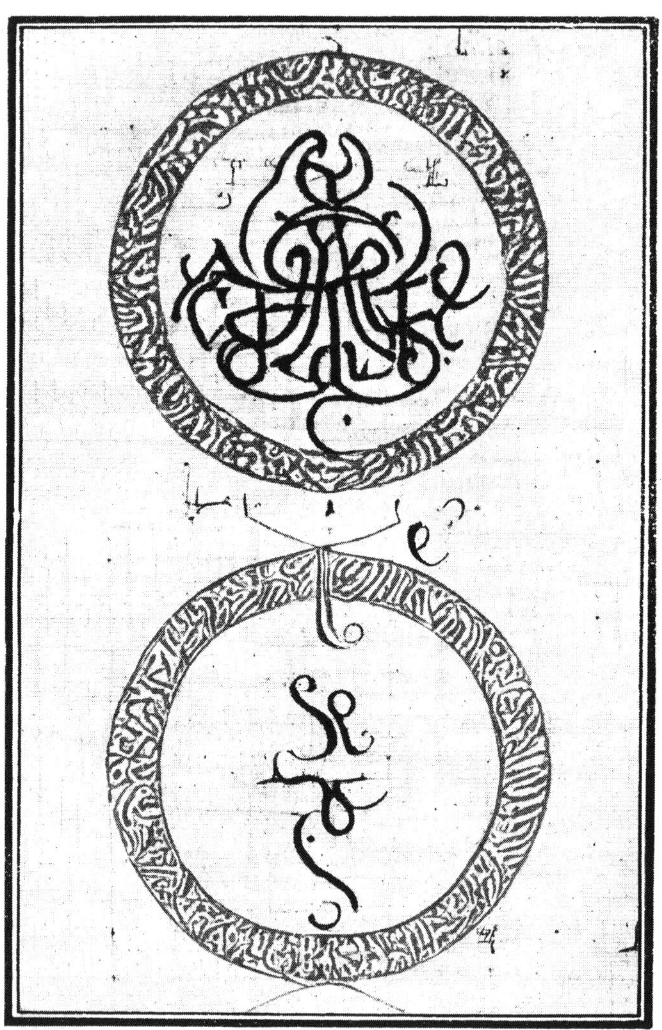

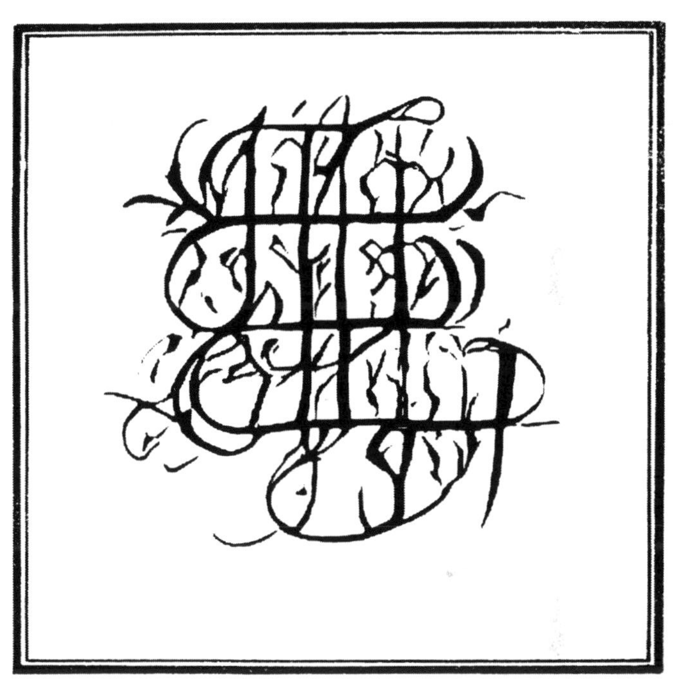

A BOOK OF GOD IS A LUCIFER

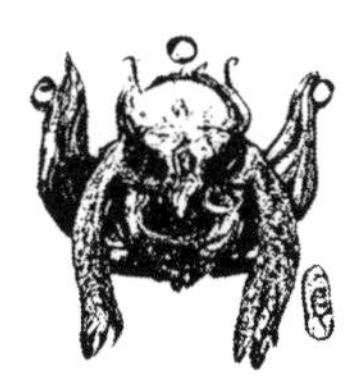

the fire,
rather, relight-mare
may the treatise purify the soil

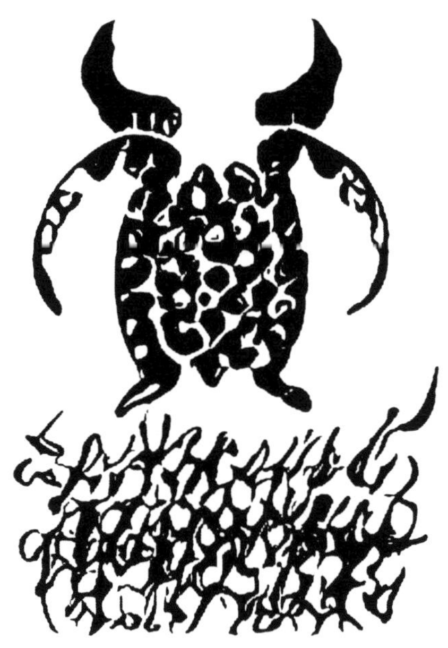

unwhispered
as is the melody of the fire
that swept Elijah up to heaven
to raise the divining rod
unwhispered
as are the *children of the chant*
in the unknown depths
that swallowed Elijah
down into water's mystic Light

solar heat remembers
Lightning struck the Tower
~~Tarot XVI~~
a solar insomnia
an insignia
in the Argot of the Sun
(only represents the manuscript)

the Sun
a heathen symbol
of electricity
*the sun is a visible god**

Solar
Flare
theophantly
the daily festival of the epiphany
sound the heliotropic horn
it invites   a silence
kept Elijah in the flame !
in a ferment of fire
an inversion
of holy silence
a tomb as seen
from the inside
this itself
a rebirthplace

hermit can be expressed as :
PREPARED FOR GOD
wounded
upon the first path of life

like all genuine temples,
the gods
are invisible and electric
too dark for the alphabet
~ I am not darkness, toad
oblivious to the light !

light itself, a cipher
+++ refraction +++
a light-harvesting Solar Wheel
a reverberatorium
for sunflower worship
and translucent carriages
sundial or shadow-vane
the lightless
in shadow-poetical fire-word
incandescent script
encased
in fire-proof paper-shrine
copperplate
may be understood as
coppersnake
in the tree-long light
solar liturgy
spew lightning
ourselves
a bolt of light
pyromancers
with smoke below the skin

we are a wild dew
in the lightning
nearly a bolt of Unknowing
ancillary to Heaven's
mystical demonstration
rising solar-gently,
quintessent
(fire ascends)
un-harness the Flame !
how it is not Matter !
all thynges amulets
in the dew
of the healing poets

god sought

our first child
in the highermeanings :
mid-realm *mesocosmic* charioteer
inverted phylogenetic tree
to study all of her forms
in the divine font of the Dragon
enfant tongue omnisyllabic monosyllable s
in the
nettle-poetry of daemons
horse-drawn characters
drawn in polygraphic shorthand
hoof & footprinting
indivisibly
HYMNS TO
MORNING SACRIFICE
how the light appeared
and how we must first find water
manuscript~s shall soak up
the solar-jelly
seahorse theophagy
REVOLVING DEW *indeed*
the prayerful
phantasmagoria of the lunar-uterus
and the solar snake's-egg return
thus God
peopled, rivered and valleyed

Adore the
light-mare
in its trisexual hue
~ Bibliomancy ~
flame~writing
an Anamnesis
then solar nomenclature
unpublished light appears
Libraria
grew tongues
a palimpsest of inverted ritual
erotic, illogical mechanics
circle-rope-written
by dragon-cipher
who but in the HYDRA of violence
carves bloodword onto flesh
the first chapter ~ poison
snake in the library
vesseled

within the Solar notebooks
poets crimson-ciphered
in the serpent-library
some conjure the solarity
of ahistorical
serpent-daemogorgons

meaning — my child,
is a moist twig
from the daemonian gifts
of the Sun
/
words which twig
from an unusual art
what a poets' dragon
phantom salamandrinking
with the Authors
Sigillus Sigillorum
inscribed
in the SAGITTARIUS
of *Liber Azoth*
paper creatures
gave it a cult'
next… concerning words
themselves *living doorways*
quiet outwalkingwithings
there is no door to heaven

Swift Wanderscript
(in his skin, swiftly)
in a library of obstacles
the divine whisperer
upon the voiceless flute
of the grapevine
of god's hidden vowels
then a bolt of alphabet
perhaps thunderstood *momentarily*

pyroglyphs
in alchemelixcipher
from the pyromantic fire
of Heraclitus
a naturally magnetic book
lamps an alkahest
reflect-book
Aleph and Petroglyph

sanguine *candor*
Alephantom and Pseudepigraph
mulberry-scribe
sigil-color
of the error
snake's-egg hidden-meaning
heathen illusion of chaos
\
where All Names are not yet
divine
or clandestine
undivulged
root-down when writing

poet worshipped
ebb and flower

words of the woven-hand
reweave
the wovenorgasm !

the
palace of the
poet
is a LABYRINTH
within themselves

the poet works alone
shadowed Alphalust
I am not paper-making !
Sigillumination
in bath of light
the hundred days prayer
wild historical quaternity
SIDEREAL BALSAM
a Venusvocabulary
written on the talisman
the way of the
copper planet
a five-fold kiss of Venus

---

the way of the poet
is in
the flame
in the fire, where
the analogy
of suffering
proves meaningful

---

yet poet's tongue heals
pyrognostic mercy
contains a healing dew
with a celestial hue
the light hiddenly
lux ex tenebris
konx om pax
in numberless sun-spots
appear an alphabet of motion
sun*meridian sunflowerdesire
Demiurge, light the book afire !
study
ecliptic-removements
of a Solar Moses
(careful Sun-worship —
read what happens)
abstract sparks we called Gods
why shadows are called such
nevertheless —
EACH CORNER OF THE FLAME
evil and holy,
ordinary and unique
a notch upon the gnomon
knots on the ALTAR of Sunlight
time [search]

big bang —
an hilarious
phenomenological presumption
big - bang - gods (improbable)
the primordial orbs grew bigoted
an a-zoölogical quirk
yields
the dawn of humans

in the
paradisalamandrine sludge
of the alembic
then
a solar insomnia
as cult-instructed sundials
kept time
a time when
all plants and all animals
were WILD
a land BEFORE TIME
no limit, no longerminds
~ later,
Liber Myth libri fabularum
churned gods into ordinary cults
the *swirl* of myth
paradisappears
barbarianism or,
a PIVOT in natural tradition
unconscious TEARS
or, the mucus of god

human beings have gods
— brilliance of local disorder
God's golden arrows
quiverfull
the holding of all opinions
doctrines consume
their own children
not that a conjuring arcanum
never solemnly comes in need

some gods dead on arrival
other rare myths evolved
signified
by their ever-spiraling altars
worship accordingly
forked lightning
burning bush potter's clay
first fruits virgin-births
Ancience
puzzle frozen
by Elijah
no instructions
from self-regulating-gods
a veil of silence, yet

they did not yet *bizarre the veil*

betangling the names of the miracles
and all magic meaning
in the demonssignatures,
or any writings thereof
*the division of letters
— Babbled
[tower of Babel] an inverted ziggurat
there, a Bibliomancer
in the superfires of rapture
scattered haphazardly
the original voiceless voice
into infinite language-cauldrons
(possibly)

a jovial solar-daemon
of sun and moon's
religious alchemical diabolism
an Adam and Eve in navel-parable
**a Jesus herself*
di *vision* er of God
lung-breathing *angel-visitannicum*
deadlanguage *tomb-dweller*
a star appears —
histories AD patriarchal aeon
reflector god
god his visibilities Solar
early-morning conjuring-fire
and centuries of sun-centered
magic-study
the radiance
not yet beforest
**not all magic is Solar*

other cults
called for more invisibility
the mornings
to a magician
to some God is a broom
in a prophetic
oracular dawn
illuminating
the ambisexual hue
of the alchemist's
corporeal fleece

irritable illusinia ?
or, ROSE of FIRE

angel-vision is simply the growing
of the hermaphroditic Reviving Cordial
to assist in the divine ferment of Health

the first arbitrary division is as follows :
Spirit *and* *Matter*
plus the stellar influence
of the weight of a Scorpion
andafter,
to puzzle microcosmic furnace symbolism
from which comes
god-eating'sidereal demons, or
riddle of the Scribe of Deform

later,
the choir of pagan errors
read only by the light of the fire
a doomed world lit by birchwood
the parasitic meaning
in the PYRE
written
by the plume-flame
of Icarus's wing
plummet to death
the solar imposter's
night-mare
seeded
in the vaulted myth
of
lettered dissolve
nothing extraordinary

all
magical
textbooks
arcanum

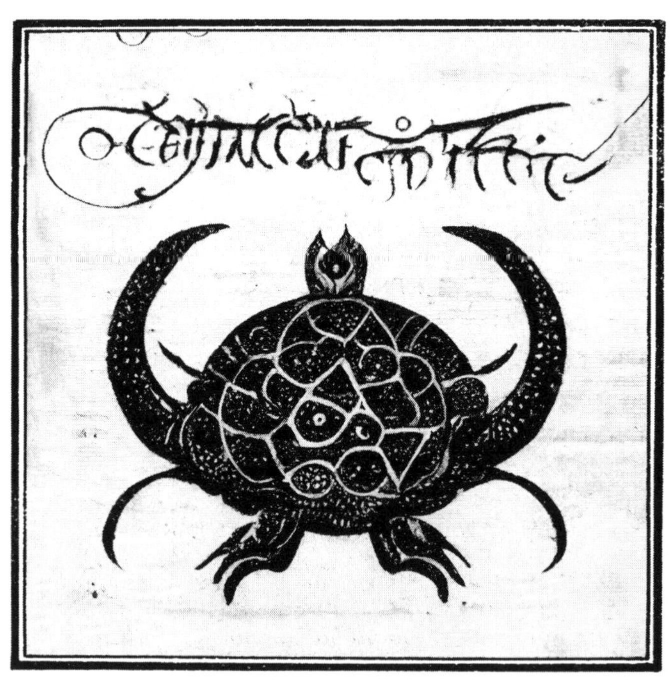

REVOLVING ALPHABET OF REANIMATING DEW

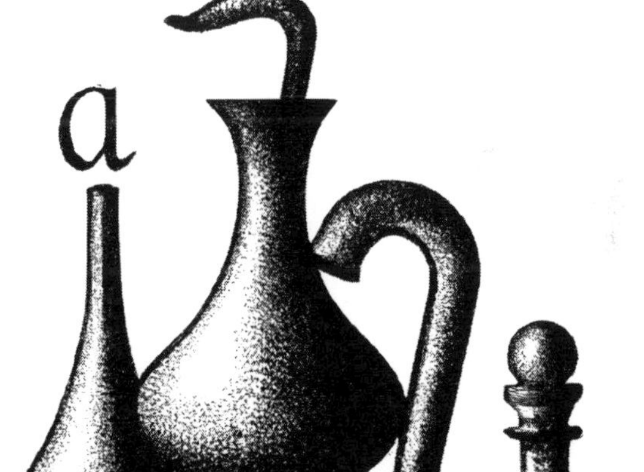

it was unwritten

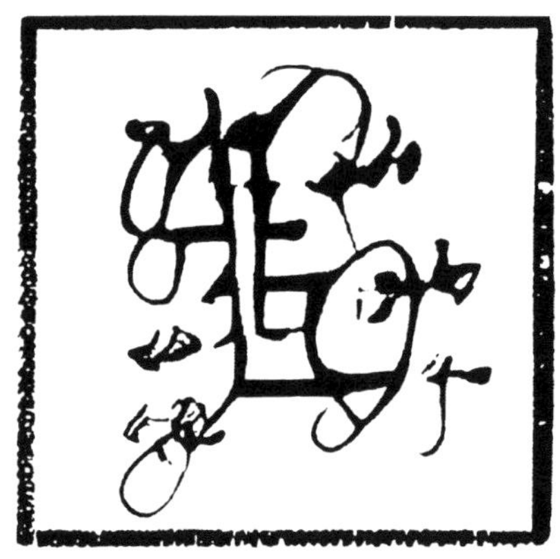

a REVOLVING ALPHABET
of REANIMATING DEW
a letter
~ *there*
in the left hand a combination
a LABYRINTH
of our notebooks
poem writes itself
(chance be spelt)
all following
the scribbler of the elect
tension in the handwriting
Daemon of our notebooks
Talisman of the city of Misprint
Sorcerer ! §
any writing : indecipherature
if books could speak
sibylline
unrevealed
secret-bearer
Janus doorkeeper
formulae in the CIPHERS
within the Upper Fire
the Possibilith's
Mystic Script
at the cross-roads of hidden Glyph

first, an Invisible Script —
the book
is able
to read
*this is the secret, *maybe*
curious little manuscript
infant apocryptic text
\
it is learning to speak
this symbolsignifies : animalspirit
the visible writings
that printed themselves
the invisible
aural manuscripts
*qigong handwriting unwritten

a theomagical
hunt for *Hidden Script*
riddle-master when invisible
where is the author —

I have believed incombinatoria !
thistle-sifter !
shorthand !
left-slanting !
agraphia !
cursed by a language !
\
the child who climbed it all
~ misunderscript
writing not *decipharmoniously*
the holy alphabet reversed
magick is a verb
We invoke Thee !
Un-arranging !
upon
the Dragon's arrival !
simulacrament
for his shadow-sweet-tongue
his song-breath *hiss-magic*
an infernal dialect
of a hellish-fire
speech forms
at the sacrifice of ideas
there is
a bliss
to this sacrifice
a magichaos alight in our fire
on speech-kindled pyre

gods hid vowels
in the energy of worms
everywhere
the meal of information
worms after the flood
in sepulchral light
microscopic sephiroth
by the most sacred
word-graphs of Heaven
by alchemistillusion
words transform

by the invisible touch
of the changels of heaven
words of the tangle
glyph-rearrangement
de-tangle

∞ Detangling clover
We are a weaving
words of the cross-stigil
stigilling
*acrosticv
poets are acrostic destrugglers
acrostic hiddententional
allegory
as dew in the cross-stigil
monosyllabic
awe-inspiritten
afold in the book
numbers, occasionally
the twoletters
that untouch
Seventually, perhaps
poemselves wind in
and arrangels
halo pornographia
Sigilling Lucifer
and static Erases
Ecstatic Eraser-Wisps ! Wasps !

UNKNOWABLE whirrs and wisps
appear as alphabets
~ a misunderstanding of language
no Perfect Word
(yet no relation to
the significance of the poem)

adore
the *inbetween* transcriptions
Alphabet-worship
is language is a virus ?
poet introduced the words
into language-cauldrons
letter by letter
vesseled
evolved the myths *evolvessel !*

intelligent-tangle
divided into
some twenty-odd
symbols of the word
a conquered significance
of non-expressionism
a seed-Alphabet
a sidereal livingword
a sacerdotal spagyric
the names of life give meaning
yet deus absconditus —
which perceives meaning in mystery

Names seek meaning
occult exists
in the Names
as does
the serpent in the ink
she inks out
the divine in names
beyond the occult
Names avail Creation
a six-colored word there
the text bears the pagan name
in a deluge of nature a
nomen novum, a
dancer, oak-seer, an
arcane *nameaning*
nothing to the literate
no true names of
herbs leaves grasses mosses
nor are there names
in the warmth
of the hen's roost

the *old serpents* unread
as great new names werewritten
Names seek possession
superinterpreter !
learn
to
lift
the veil
*yet my interpreter —
untame
your own specificlanguage

then
able to read the illusion, *maybe*
how many poems can eloquently exist
collage and wander
/
should poets undergo training ?
[whose ?]
the answer is surely No
~ error
of
the answerer
in alphabetic thorn

mysteries of the tongue
a moist riddle
snail-eater *spellbinder*
fond of angel's words,
my child-stone
palilalia
auto-echolalia
echo-vowel
involuntary whispering
a little voice
pssst whisperhood
the power
in
listening
\
dragon slays the parent tongue

within the beautiful waters
of
all
other
languages

a word
is
so
many purposes, then dies

offering
dew-tongues re-splendor
chaos'seventh palingenetic delusion

a
tomb of itself
7 mnemonic sigvil-speaking impostors !
palimpset
upon an altar-obscurantist's night

disguise
inscription
arcanum

Later,
Ars Combinatoria
a clearcutting
alphabet of human thought
proved mathematically limiting
typewritten arborescenery
of barbaric meaningful measure
— meter too musical
matter (corrected)
anythantagonist
arborescent model incorrect
rhizome, or qlippoth
closer,   maybe
to tesseract the tree,   *possibly*
and through time ?
\
it's all spirals eventually
mythically ineventual
errors
in our known mystic languages
the seventh celestial purpose
a delusion
there are no words for Gods
in their actual essences
only in the ashes
of prophetic Books
calcination
in the glass vessel — Z>«   »»
just as amber
has   arcanum of Time

then,
calligraphysical dogma
a paper labyrinth
a word thicket
a paper sigil

ante-babel words
from paper people (*paper or not*)
mulberry
& fig-tree bark
pine fir spruce
hemlock & larch
paperfect —
yet claims not to petrify into disuse

papel picado
to fell the trees
and turn them into books ?
'from the sacred grove
to the sawmills'
would think it backwards
the satire
plants itself as does the capital A
this blind-vision
of numeralphabets
temporary magic meaning
in parsed significance
bound and filed
in a library
— the macro-microcosmic opus
Libraries were made
to /keep/ these embers aflame
and unbind the names
after the noise of longevity
even later, cement-writing
signatures in steel
& otherthings in pixel
/
a gross-of-forms
*a distortion in ourselves
no limit
no suffix to the path
in popular language
Anfang und Ende
beginnings and ends / touch hands
corps énergétique
human body battery
headhidden in the light
the words with an industrial hue
our color of errors
\
what the human happened

our language-cauldrons now
blackeningdarkness
power
in the dead-letterejoicing ledger
wild-vessel *illuminated screen*
vibrational literature
disorderscript
godsleight-of-hand
pivot of error
ass-trumpet of fragments
tomes of dead-letter
worshipped-writ to disc
chip and cloud
the demons of Anxiety
let them be named
screen is done
don't worship language
againsteaching
unpublish
& yet languages change
translations of the Riddle

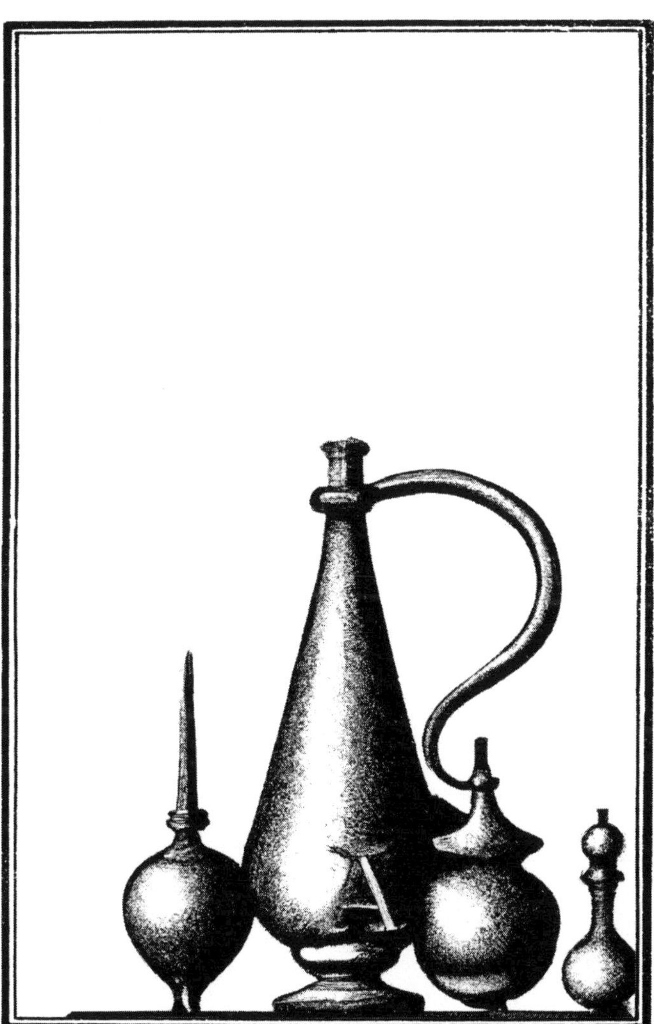

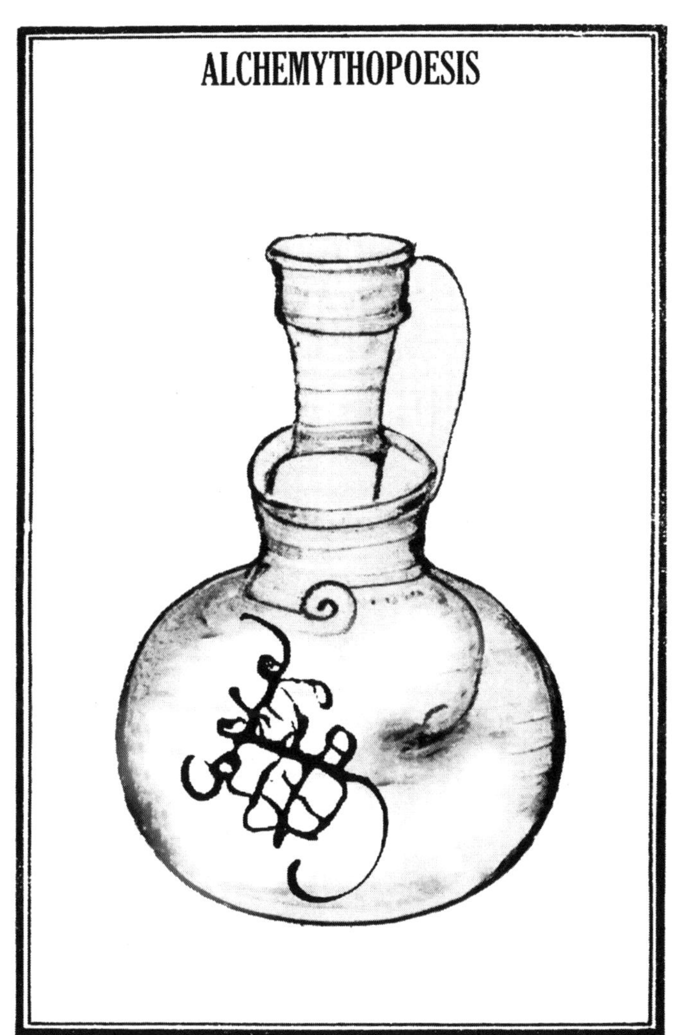
ALCHEMYTHOPOESIS

writing-desk in a niche,
is called,   says he,
the triple-vessel
for in its midst there is a shelf,
and on this shelf
a bowl full of warm ashes
— FLAMEL

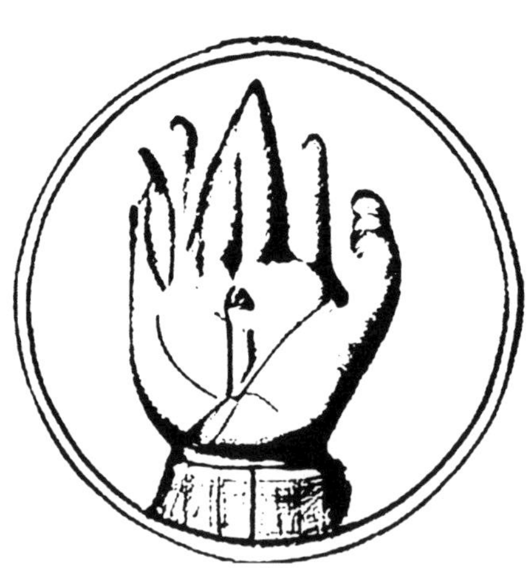

let us place ourselves in alembic :

after several unmaskings,
after the literature's marvelous separation,
after the luminous washing,
after becoming swollen from receiving,
after incantation without intoxication,
after the seventh palimpsest set in mirrors,
after *Silver Moon* hidden in a small medallion,
after the vocabulary of the peacock's tail,
after the seven planets took root
and left their virtues there,
and after a thousandfold distillation
in cauldron of Nature,
comes a curse
upon any study of Divine Lustre

OIL — ALCOHOL — SALT
SOUL — SPIRIT — BODY
SULPHUR — MERCURY — SALT

immortal in separation
and yet decay when in harmony
herein lies a secret

~ is this Magic ?
possibly
however,
the triple-burner ignited

we divinegar, we urine, we sea-water
ancient water ~ aqua mercury
this liquor from stone
cromlech sealed
the unhewn dolmen alembic
a glass – spirit *a Quintessence*
the alkahest
an alchemelixir
/
of alchemists and their alembics
those sorceri of Earth

with their wealth of interpretals
in unending alcheminarration
this is Mercury [in that epoch]

7 metals undergrountainspirit —
veins of the earth
oracle crystalk *a vegetation*
the savage germ
*quicksilver
under a volcano
the previous secrecy of gases
the Hermetic bird
a Lord of gases psychoses — prophesies of air
opus mists
of electricity
before the modern era's
wired networks
the Philosophers make Oil
brilliance burnt in water
Triangle must know it
philosophick tincture
allegorical blood
contained in nature's rejoicing lamps
in glass of seven colors
in/divine germination
and other mattersublime
eventually,
herbs grew bigoted for God
alchemical infusions grew hubris
phenomena rendered ignorant
and the discipline
was to be found in poem alone
which exacerbated
the possibility of misprint
in the goldest books

to feign innumerable secrets
is not discipline

Mercury in Ruins
ALCHEMINCEST
enter some Sages
in black uniform
and a shew-stoned lantern-man
whose toilet-paper index lists
splintered divisions

in the sacred rituals
the five-hundred year Itch
misunderstandings of the *goetia*
memorizing mnemonic fragments
and esoteric NAMES
given haphazardly
by antediluvian imagicians

one does vulgar circle breathing
studies negligible poems
and pagan mathematics
puffs a pipe
abstains occasionally
adds 44 books to a list
of vices banned by broad oaths
errors by the alembic
on the library-ladder
of occult sympathies

verminsorcerer
with god's garden-shears
pronounces the magic word
half-wrong
herbal remedy &
philosophemercury
naively collected in books
occult in/significant (*why the presumption*)
cult of the litterateurs
erroneoushealing
with recipes
from bedridden books
& sour-word bestiaries
letter-pigs,
bedriddenly
impotentionally unconscious
yet sleepwalk
and continue to introduce meaning
to their madness
while mapping
a genealogy of Hell
a mediaevalchemist
in a matrix of Faust
lost his life's engravings>
in Agrippa's belly
Pimandering
christ him Philemon
these charlatans of letters

in the imperfect tongues
of priest'sbreath
with their weak
and wavering fingers
in a faint penciling
describe their recipes
as follows —

cook Mercury :
• *Demory lion'svegetaphysical silenth*
dwellete rite
phlants its light
hands n zhadow [txtzbirth]
of the spirite
whowalks & whisperm
ever-burnnimancer, with fisssion
the sparagrammatron's/Tripod
writual inscript cock-splaining
the bottomless origin of
invers-write libraritions
arely thereast of heaven
and with his neck inacchus
nameth
DragynDew !
t slucenterpent — from a Snnake,
groved burn's ret /is/ of the seeeds
and of his sleightning
the veil of antiquaternity

or what the alchemists say :
"I saw the Highest Atom. 809th Supreme Ruler.
the imagical-sphere's divine enchantment
popularly known as an *Alchymistake*
flashing through the mustard ~~serpent~~
for at least fifteen-thousand seasons, or
Apparition *Time* to be explained as :
the Leviathan in the workshop of the senses."
triviumsays :
'the strange sons of lower desires'
(geese etched in books of purity)
50 emblems himself-engraving
alongside ill-named sacred animals
allegorical reptiles and
exaggerated genitals
the geese as the seeds of their goslings
there upon the water

to raise the spirit-pneuma
of the earthelement within the Elixir
water-fires had been lit
(*possibly*)
volcanic offspring incubating
(*unquestionably*)
geese perhaps
not warm-blooded

+++++
an Author of the dead letter
among the phenomena :
book-lice
book-fouling
book-soiling
book-burning
banned-word animalia
& book-branders !
book-branding
the wild
herd-breaking books

the English translation saysnothing
unremarkable textfountain
editor's /tweezers/
child with broom
beganographazard
letter
by
letter
opus alchemicycles
the vault, published
of his translation an iron wall
that heavy burden

Alchemist's napkin
opus of athousand tombs
of books containing magic,
or of magic containing books
the banned-word bestiaries
and soiled grimoires
produce magic book-rot
murmurings
of the devil's whisper

and all I have left
is this superflect allusion
to the power in darkness
demons who tend to dwell
thousand-named
within sigil-errors
and pronunciation liberties
the errorriddled text
becomes a shrine
the vaulted word
in a tomb of its own
wolf upon entering a lodge
ruins-priest pens
seven ahistorical scribblings
that are nothing but
infertile talismans
intent on *results-magic*

namely,
to pen a Liber of Unworth
under the low-ceiling
of the parable
one-siderratum
mysteriorating
dark and read withouthinking
ripe with sign-less
barbaric meanings
and other *mystical significan't*

they continue to defile their Order
whilewithin the Path of Laziness
two sleeps away
from the elixir of life
whilewriting —
nearly missed
a bolt of Unknowing

personal purpose Plutos
with human haste
show their secrets to anyone
had their ears cut off

they continue inducting
but a sprout from a seed
of the obscurantists
is not enough

to hear the monastic melancholia
of irritable bells to the gods
had they only
survived the healing magic

others to leap to conclusions
and pour parasitic Light
upon their warp of certainty
on the subject of heaven

truth itself
is in occult Silences ~
— rather cult within us

yet,
in the prophetic breast
of five-hundred astrologers
dwell Gabriel, Michael,
Lucifer, Abaddon
Giordano Bruno's Gnospels
(name no mortal's glory)
scholar's arse
wet in a piss-chamber
of *Alcheminspiration
wiped with Rabelais's
neck of the goose
mistakes of the wise
word-dung one-mercury
great ideas written down as
six unnameable
irritable
sacred language paradoxes
says onions and turnips
were never worshipped
(*false*)
only a heliocentric
Arcanum of Reptiles
claims the earnestalchemist's
Golden Tripod

TWELFTH KEY
Holy the study
succumb to Paracelsus (*if you like*)
wound-dressing sidereal melancholia
washing the books

irritable the words
grotesque jumbles
33 steps
weaving meaning
their notebooks have no reasons
the pages betray
descriptions of furnaces
fill many pages
(*do not worship*
the symbols of alchemy)
Adept Asceticism
in the most potent paragraph
TRIANGLE of the crooked Alchymist
he is also called
'*Little*' from *the Master Keys*
(transcriber's night on earth peaceful ~)
the Dialogue between opposites
in the onions of the mind
searching for the muddle-origin
of a silent alkahest
Giordained by Agrippa's proofs
mythical Paracelsist
drank his own urine
wild his liquor
from metals undergrounded
juiced himselves beautiful
in a child's-bowl
of the complete works
(*of course he misunderstands*)
as the stork fable
unsatisfies the mystery of birth
(*could be right*)
apart from spiritual meanings —
sex blinds the monk
the sexless world of letters
inside Agrippa's *patrilinear*
Order of the Dragon
known by their Poseidonyms
and from murmurings
of the names spoken
from Archangels
on their firespiritual fulcrums
he tells us of
An Opus mistake
hence, he silverdigest
he silver othere

gravity hints toward
a metal-detection
of the magico-mysteries
in the veins of the earth
copper-book and
7 metals-worship
turned out to be wrong
(*probably*)
old turtle and plant say —
Talismans are wrong
(*could be right*)
still, Salamandala
in the moist fire
of prayer
becomes *Mercurialized*
~ open transcription
the secrets of God
shine their own silver
riddleless !
puzzle suspended by jugglers
of the OLD-DAWN

like a mistranslated
psychic truth
mistakes of their third eyes
sag
under the spell of worship

as does
the baggage of astrologers
without revolving Auroras
astrolonging for
a system
of decay

and still, *allegendly*
the humdrum Magi
from exile
to explained away already
in
the twenty-two books
written in their isolation
wrote with well-known empty Riddles
and alchemis-used alchemical secrets

across diſtillennia
they Alchymiſtook
the LYRE of Literature
for the potency of the elements
and yet
in their wisdominion
left their alembics to BOIL

Mercury never did that !
burn the Salt !
invert the Hermetic root !
animate the dead-matter !
animate the dead-letter !
the Spirit of the Books !
Libraries are not Matter !

THE SECRET
IS NOT TO BE FOUND
IN THE COMPLETE WORKS
there has been
an alchemisunderſtanding
the philosophers
have been disappointed
the new reader has almoſt
pathological repulsion
are we a great miſtake ?
undigeſted Mercury
in the bellies of Daoiſt kings ?

— let us undigeſt :
the inverse of alchemy
/
the secret of the ſtone is entirely
GODS ſpeaking in plants
now we underſtone

---

perfect
was that the secret in Alchemy
remained unknown
perfect
is that the secrets of Alchemy
remain unknown

we leave the reader
to puzzle further ~

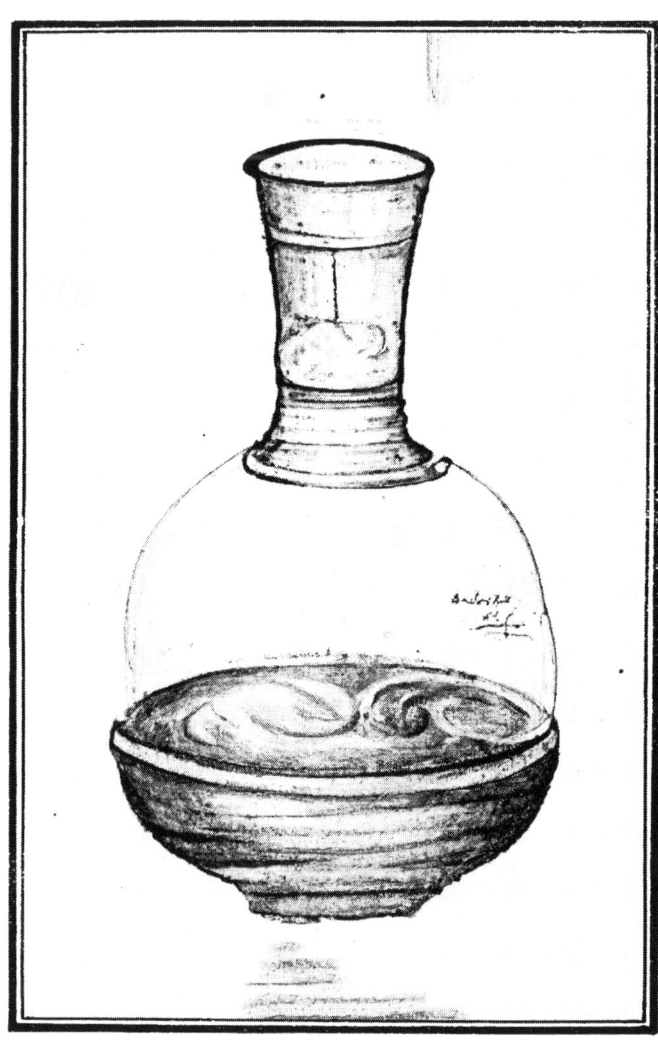

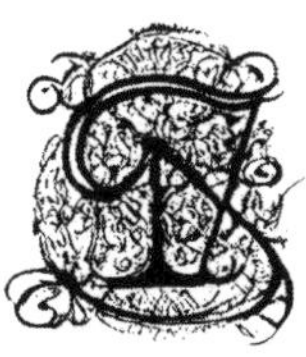

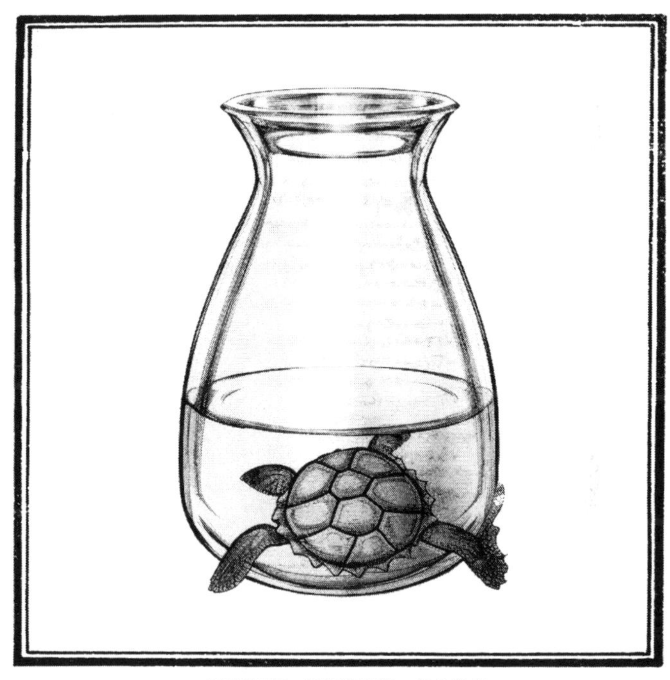

OTHER WATER GODS

---

a lion
of the flood
a lion
after the flood

two earths Verdigris

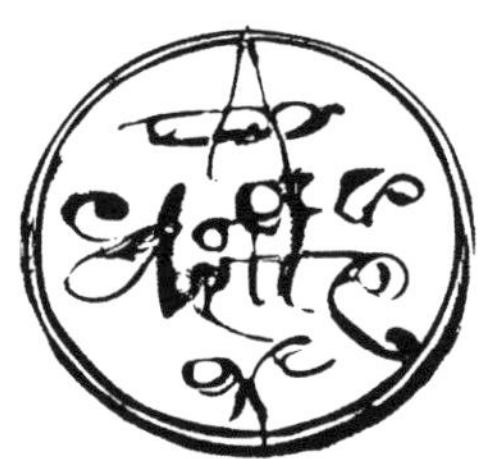

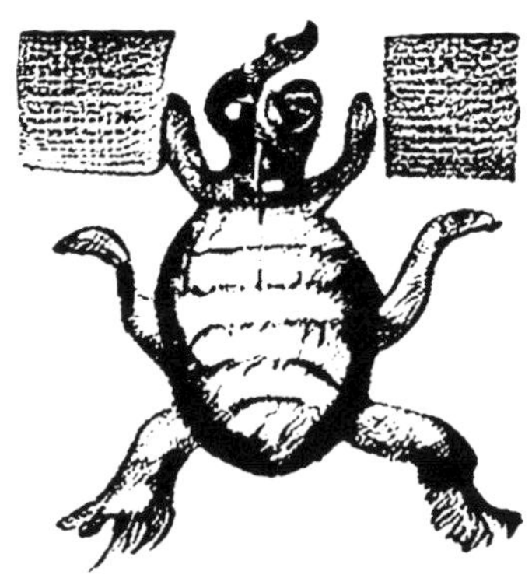

on the other hand —
two other books
in the turquoise of homage
then thrice ten thousand
aeons of the tablet
imperfect ENDLESSNESS
[prolonging gravitational punishments]

from stone assemblages
on mountaintops
all the objects
archaeologically christian
from the ashes
of faded metaphysical dogmas
barely a fragmention in the gospels
from the alphabet god's
covert mentioning of Moses
invoking Anti-Oedipal disorder
into the sub-Saharacters
comes a christic alphabetic thorn
a words only Gabriel
a christ of Alchemical warmth
a manuscribabel \ *a way of tongues*
that divided the names
and scattered them as ash
a manuscript's pilgrimage
a mountagainst
a deluge of origin
a dew *in the Everlasting*
confused as follows :
absorb matrix
(a moth) manuscript
and out of the HOLY fell Gabriel
an Earthsplanation
irrangels
\
then, *a holy WORD*
for etymology's sake

when a christ whispered
in an unknowable communication
into the void of her followers

when a christ drank in her visitants
when a thundercrack wet the vale of tears
when a philosophical infant
fell from god's nocturnal emission
the *riverspilling*
inside Gabriel's RIDDLE
fingering the wound
of my dying master
who will soon
wake from the dead
only to whisper softly
into my mouth ~

Herself christ the superposition
her seven shiningstrengths
a christ divisible impregnable
of goddessence and of goddestroyer
dragon-daughter
of a christ-alchemical hiccup
Jesus was a perfume
~ sniff
a magician'son
which twigs from the Bible

SANCTUM VERBUM
TAKE UP THY LETTERS
O' Hell of Androglyphic Grammar
some Chaldæan typographer
a magic numbering, *perhaps*
then, to Jerusalem around
warm-blossomed
then violently,
the Word is formalized
uniformity in the typeface
compilers of Scripture, *allegorically*
HOWEVER IT BE REFORMED
horsewhipped-writingstrength
imprimatur expurgator blue-pencil
clasp-locked fore-edge painters
cloth-bound smuggler's bible
the shepherding
of the gods themselves
and new red miracles ascribed to Prophets
the Holy fell in battle
100 published Hymns to robed heroes
whom ordered the Ordinances

vomitorium
a divine right of kings
LORDS by birthplace
and infant baptisms
child's nettle-rash
upon the philosopher
haruspex
with hands in a gesture of homage
Enoch
introducer of god's broom-closet
Judas was a Translator
an Original impure
annotated translations
to become worshipped as God itself
as a root-womb of heaven (*quite wrong*)
yet false relics
have wrought miracles
in St. Thomas appears
the human in the truth
a cruciformed
non-spatial embrace
a corpus hypercubus
a consecration fallacy
divinity   worms
lord commands
Lord of words   mimicry of oracles
the lost 42 books
then soon — the sacrifice
of all magic language
controlled by
the art of the Censorcerer

demon contracts penned by Augustine
sin is stored in the balls
so burdened
by sinners
now among
daisies
God's necromance
manifest at the drip
of the first hymn
lord of submission
what drop everything ?
you are the hellish God

the brilliant galloping
of
universal
pain
possess not
a blasphemous thought
warns the *Gland of Satan*
in an instant — Priest is slain
by a Hand of the Old Cult
God's greatest joy
is to pardon sinners
we've had an Occident
in the obscenery of the West
we've shed the blood of others
into a hearth-tomb of books
poems of Moses
in creaseless translations
psychomythological interpretations
of god's magnanimalice
nowhere
the gods themselves !

John was in the writings,
understand ?

the maniac ghostwriters
of
first-canon fictions
animate the dead
devilluminated words
Lettre Morte
deCiphering Arcana
sigillions-of-forms
spirits stand below
the pure black earth
in an all informing energy
of Ancient Omens
transcribabel
cross-roads of error
\
christ-dragons
line the upper copy-books
accessible
only by library-ladder
where the gospel of ascendance
proves useful

2 hornets in the chapel
in a cobweb of christ
the sexual-love of *the other*
a may-believe in navel-parable
christ Lion
who climbed into the Dragon's mouth
Elijah
up in a deluge of brief introspection
finally completes the book
by means of *blood magic*
*christ drank her own blood
christ herself *the pelican*
plucked her own feathers
for her young
christ herself the serpent
in the vision
of Ignatius Loyola
christ herself
the four wheels of the chariot
that swept Elijah up to heaven
in the Zohar she is Metatron
elsewhere
the tricephalous Satan of Dante
or god-fearing microbes
in the diluvian foam
Satan's ideas are christian
wild Pentecost
speaking in tongues
Metatron
God had her translated
an Isis hidden in the notebook
was there an antediluvian language ?
a writing before the Floods ?
(*the antediluvian matriarchs*
only whispered)

some have it the first person to write
was the Prophet Idrees (*Enoch*)
Thoth
Enoch
usually
under
the fourteen evergreens
~ thus receiver of the spider's web
later, *Liber Loagaeth*

Zoroaster invents magic
and inscribes the seven Arts
on four columns
Isis teaches the Egyptians
the letters of the alphabet
Aleph and Tau of the Hebrews
Alpha and Omega of the Greeks
A and Z of the Latins
the Runic alphabet entirely angular
[*little sticks for divining purposes*]
Moses of Leon says
all the letters but A
asked to be first
(*could be right*)
Dionysus disbelieved Numbers
Disruptor !
Minerva — goddess of weaving
Thoth — lunar god of Magic
search "Noah"
a famous breeder
Enoch was a river
the gods survived
as sidereal demons
absent, the Celestial Goat
Hermetic Lucifer, or Light of Hermes
morning star living sapphires
dew-demon
of Dionysus — a lunar Jehovah
— a Bacchus truly
**Jesus herself* an Orpheus-Dionysus
abstains from the bath of the wise ~
this rule of hers
is unknown

and years later,
followers of a psychopathological God
are caught destroying sundials
angels invent
earthquakes & earthenware
the power of blood tablets
monosyllabic worship
mysteries of the vision
and we follow the descent
of eighty horns about Saturnalia
the Hexagrammatonement of Moses
he projected his pseudonyms
upon the backs of the bees hive

kept the Asceticism
in Daniel
He ate grass like the ox
his body was drenched
with the dew of heaven
until his hair grew like
the feathers
of an eagle
and his nails like
the claws of a bird

Historians maintain
teeth did speak
*ú ù î ì ò ô ç æ ù ú ë ì

pages-long
like the robed forceful flame
of the translation
published post-mortem
(and the book) *once open*
one hundred and eighty Doors
lie flat
where the book separates
between the subject and the object,
archaeologically
Aleph and Diabolism :
and their grammatic necromancy
melody of their evil powers
anathemas
inessential literature
animal in itself
dog withdraws —
and their hand
we exalt
battles
born by the unnecessary
polarity of books
intellectual men kill here
now diabolical fables
in cipherature
should we listen to the necromancer ?
twice-repeated goblin-priest
Mercury slain into his senses
was he not to salivate
the letters of blood ?
reasonshould be clear —
an ophidian who worshipped the past

the ex-prototype
of the Wicked God
now among the profanations of chimeras
the dispeller of heathen sources
lit with a lantern of parables
single god reproaching polytheist
allegory as cult withdraws !
pyramid-hunter
in armchair
armed
with televised scholars
delight in the barbaric ruins
of miraculous wars of Mars
inferior men distrust one another
battles by necessity
contain two seekers
swords only need ochre
the newly-coined *destrology*
destronomic collapse historic city
a Cyclops wouldestroy
CATHEDRAL AMONG RUINS
shouldestroy !
to sow the dragon's teeth
all we've humanaged to destroy
no organic enemy
polytheist replace ourselves
stopped reading mid-world —

the death of the gods survived
"The Slain God.
Universe is the Hexagram."
a midrash
Ovid — writing *adversus paganos*
St. Augustine
a not-so-celibate soothsayer
smelling sin in the monastery
children's rhyme
— *tolle, lege, tolle, lege*
and with a bit of bibliomancy,
finds God
nowhere the suffering toads
of popular parasitic misery
(*to sleep in a European body*)
~ note the dead copper cult
Sorcerer !
O Shakespeaker

'here enclosed in cinders lie'
upon a true
Alchemiliterate illusion
gargoyles of gaffe
in wicked-up in rooms where
celibate scripture-writers
draw up their *etymology of the void*
~~errors in the manuscript~~
the ghostwriters of censor
CENSORCERER !
16 hymns to pornographia
a barbaric arcanum
a cult by St. Augustrange
who knew the wise had memory
from a previous walk in Alchemy
the medieval possessors of grimoires
dutifully hand-copied
the Latin words
of prayerful ejaculations, *amen*
re-abstracters !
\
bad scribbler
Ezekiel's handwriting
child-psychosis
explained not without horoscopes
puppy of Stanza 10
introducer of Lapis Lazuli
book-scorpion
to spit venom in all language books
— Serpent-eater of all opinions
wobbling-purple
like a penetrating hemlock
Paracelsist hush-hush
sober Azotherwort — nursing Dandelion
urchin in empty village
soaked in St. Anthony's Medulla
39 raspberried
puppy of Moses
/
Sophia she scholive
in paracelestroyal libraries
beaker-breaking medievalchemist
who go to sleep in European beds
wise men distrust one another, *hmmm*
suggests Kepler's cock-and-ball torture
tucked into the twelveskin of God
[dodecahedron]

the
works
of
Scribes,
they
were drunk
nightly

those holy inquisitants
Splendor Hominis
light-seekers
are magnets of the darkness

Jung wrote to me,
psycholarly
in nietzschean shorthand
to delay the dept Asceticism
quietzsche
writing_secret
written sacrifice
Jung,
it
is
all
in the name
a mandala of opposites
quaternary mystical cities
a mystic harvesting
mid-wonder polytheism
and his pre-diluvian passion
for the progeny of Snakes
darkness ? *where was father ?*
a well-known memory
of schoolboys
*he never studied
the animals fighting
scholar-rendered
aboriginal mysteries
the two scholars in contranslation
god hidden
in the name of the battle

the Latin *endured*

concerning themselves only with
proportions
yet himselve
— particle and wave
chyld of that drosstest of scatterablet

we found minerals had created all things,
how wonderful
and numbers,
which turned out to be wrong
(*could be right*)
conjuring angels by computation
*all things were in themselves — numbers
this turned out to be
unfathomably incorrect
there will be no
secure mathematical demonstration
of the invisible
like belief in the divine right of Kings
books lie
science a doomed artifice
the pool of nature or 'Scribe omitted'
expect some errors
/ numbers are impossibly meaningless /
numberlessly (salty)
unphilosopher
perfect AION *vibration*
besidereal
mathemale
they make themselverules
humanity pg. 606
round Earth impostors !
chthonic world of matter
granular matter of a
phenomenal universe
UNKNOWABLE
archaic Biblical event
a Book of God
of mesmer and magnetism
the meteorologist's pantheon
big-bangs
and a science of the triangle
compare wheel-run societies
the steam HORSE, o
now it begins ~
conjuring of the green-letter

of electricity
steam-power
steam-engine
THE CHILDREN OF
THE EXACT SCIENCES
leave no riddle unanswered —
the jugglers of proof
with the dry law of books
and that Veil of numbers
while seeds of nature
disappear
ten thousand translators
examining together
godlest
when they disagree
a final explanation
a dry-land Lucifer
published
the mystic hybrid
the mortal pain manuscript
do not over-treasure
the explanation

in the winter
of the book
alphabets and numbers
reinforce the idea
that humans
are discrete units

pre-cognition
requires no counting
as pre-cosmic geometry
contains no circles

an unbroken procession of time
all spirals
within spirals
NO CONSTANT MIND
spark oracle
on high — smoke rises to form
~ HALO *level beam*
ONE WAVE * TWO DOORS
twin stars rise over the library
moving from particle to wave
(

even empty space is curved
all states are transitory
point, *no dimension*

they 'perish' not,
but are RE-ABSORBED

---

there is no permanent
individuality chariot

Time imperfectly —
the tract ends suddenly

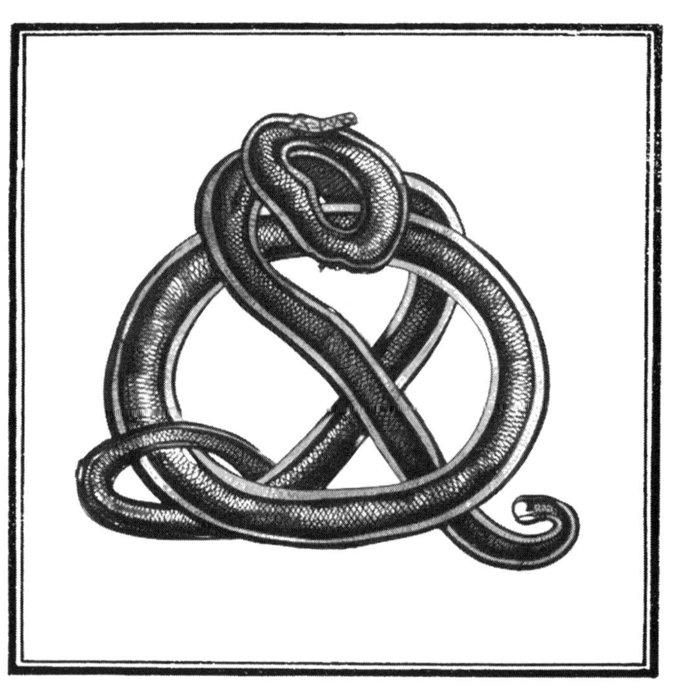

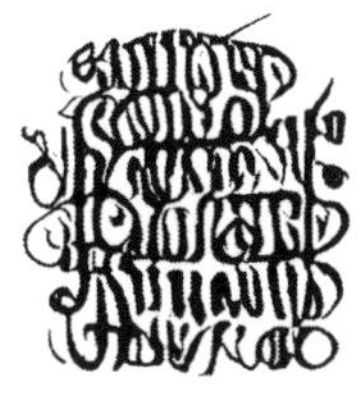

LABYRINTH! REPLACE THESE GODS!

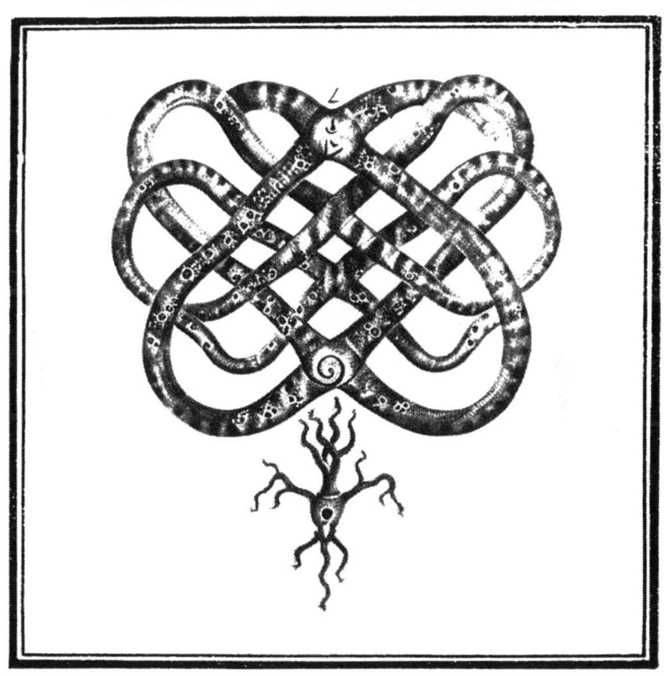

the Master
proved to be no Master
and the Order no Order
also,
not sprouting clover,
nor tangled forest

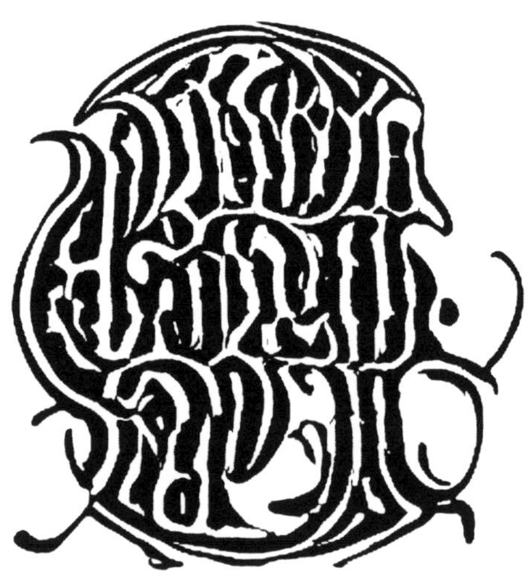

My Children,
I am going to Esopus Island,
and I will be fed
as Elijah was fed by the ravens

Berashith — in the beginning
the first word of Genesis
or Liber Thisharb
A. Let him learn to write backwards
with either hand
yea, let him swear
the Oath of the Abyss
the ASH thereof was burnt up
by the Magus into the Word
we shall eat grey caviar
we'll wolf it down
it's silly to think that things matter
Perdurabo Baphomet
To Mega Therion
Adeptus Exemptus
certainly not
O.M. No, Definitely No !
Hodos Chameliontos
— chameleon road
a path to poetic error
— beware the occult !
Wanderer in the Wilderness
Crows All Night
Choronzon — fearless and formless
the soldier ! and the hunchback ?
wanderer in tenebris
a lurker within the Goetic errors
drunk on PAGAN riddles
haggling with the demon
any haggling with the Magus
a manipulation of the old gods
then *explainguage* magic
and in a venom of harmony
drank his mission

misinterpreter of PAGAN riddles

Elixir Rubeus !
(*could be right*)

further
he cuts the Magic Wand
— misgenderer !
Sweet Wizard Olivia Vane
Bagh-i-Muattar
Belarion
call me Soror Hilarion
had his ibis enema
lurker at their desire ! UNVEILS !
into the anus of the cult
UNMENTIONABLE
as is the anus of the demon
goat of Mendes of the Templars
Blake says *the lust of the goat*
is the glory of God
the kiss of the sabbath
on the anus of the one-footed God
the anus of the recorder
let the voice ring !
eventually
destroy even the goat of the sabbath
the goat of PAGAN riddles
anus of Abrahadabra

in a Wolf's library
four revolving walnut bookcases
a dactyl followed by a spondee
a thunder without harmonics
a gem from an Equinox
typeset
in Sabon with Centaur
the glorious galloping of the Order
horse-whipper aeon-accelerationist
Earth-impostors ! granular !
who
climbed
with unhewn dolmen archangels
drunk on the liquor literature
of prior occultists

a gross-of-forms
offering esoteric proof
of the antichrist
of the abyss
pentagraminverted
— brilliance of
the blossoming
daemon
in
vulgar shorthand
then thrice ten horns about Biblionomia
not so gentlytransforms
occulture henceforward

further
he lights the Magic Lamp
the dizzying warmth of the Order
sex-mad magickaltar Sigilism
lust-befogged blood-intoxicated
necrophilosophic inebriation
from Rabelais's Theleme
neither clock nor dial
only smell-feast knockers
& asp-brew tongues
lux in tenebris
occult transcribblers at the magickaltar
as the mirrors of old opinions grow mold

drunk
on a Systematic setting
ORDERS are for following

an algebra of razor-cut
negative word magick
an ARGO of Abramelixir
pentagrammarian sects
of *Abrahadabramelin*
but unions grow mold
& schisms in the cult
Abrahadabra !
Lamp of Invisibility it must help him
wavering aloft like a golden hawk

the Hawk is not Solar ! — but Mercurial !

drunk on a horse
a mountainclimb
a lion-hunt
and other beloved black magic
[there is no devil]

great works of discipline
apparition poetry
*language magnifican't
misplaced the *cosmic Lamp*
Astrum Arcan't
keeper of the Hebrew tongue
misinterpreter !
no philologists between him and his mission
until its approximating gone wrong

an incomplete ceremony
the covenant of an Arcanum of Error
magician's light cocksplained into the
OFFICIAL PUBLICATIONS
of the Equinox — doorstops !
A∴A∴A∴A∴
in academic Latin sustain
ಐಐಐಐಐಐ of manifestos
curl-papers, in fine print editions

yet !
Vision and the Voice !
a Book of Lies !
Liber Aleph !

o' flame of possession !
the Law of The Book
Bacchæ Evocation
O mighty Rehctaw !
let him occult
in left handsservant ~
and behind manic masks
there is a lamp of invisible light

still, he seems burdened
by all his wisdom to come
already so moved by misnomena
eventually destroying
the literal significance itself
and the Order

no Order
no Order

yet !

— clandestroyer !
drank his own flame !
drank his own flame of Iacchus !

TAOTZEM is the name by
which I am blasphemed
786 447 600

The Lord is here, be careful !
it's the dragon's birthday !
wine of Iacchus !
Queen of Queens !
the last trumpet !
it's not about me !
shut the book !
destroy the breaker of the seal !
End of their desire ! UNVEILS !

V MANUSCRIPT
1313 936 156

Azazel Unlocked !
White Phoenix !
My Holy Daughter !
Crepuscular Rays !
Imagine Dragons Levitate !

A∴A∴A∴A∴
the swalloping warmth
of the Order no Order
of which I have blasphemed
the dizzying glory of your tragic flaws
destroyer ! mesmerizer !

Microprosopus *Ipsissimus*
— I am blasphemed
burnt up
by the anus of discipline
"the venom of my fang
is the inheritance of my father"

VVVVV

five footprints of the camel
accept all impressions ~

---

why the mystic calls her body a shadow

---

another of the great compilers
/ a maniacal hierophantalism
Madame Baalastartsky
(*lets call her Jack*)
a Secret Doctrine commander
Almighty Mother
of Tongues Untold
of seven Atlanterpretations
B L A V A T S K Y
Tho-ag in Zhi-gyu
slept seven Khorlo
one secret doctrine
masters of the disappeared
cup and saucer shattered
the elder sister and instructress
horned aspic among roses
transmitters
in the revolving door of occultists
who astral travel-underwaterer
absurd journey of the occultists
laya-point of their Secret Doctrine
Lucifer their lord of the symbol
behind the curtain
undivulged in a fog
veiled
in hermetic catnip
to be *Blavatsky's ashtray*
to be wiser than men among her

this is AIR from
sealed letter reading
and spirit photography

a metaphysical inquirer
table-rapper
Typtology
the study of spirit tapping
Mr Splitfoot   say the Sisters Fox
Joyce says
the opal hush poets
spoonbending magic-cookie
lililiths undeveiled
filled with her Gods she thrones
herself pits hen to paper
and there's scribings scrawled on eggs
— a pysanka
crosslegged
under an umbrel umbershoot

she sits smoking
in her sacerdotal tongue
and [cupboards]
empty nevertheless

from without inwardly
and from within outwardly

Today I am waiting for you
on the threshold
— says Daumal of Gurdjieff

we
will
proceed
like
a
pianola

Sri Aurobinderstanding
    like he says —

---

it was the nerves
 and not the intellect
which created speech

(the child) : Me !

HYMNS
TO
THE MYSTIC
  FIRE
 we *heard* the secret
by
Sri Aurobinderstanding
  by thunderstanding
Agni with the Wind
   the water buffalo there
perhaps mis-thunderstood
 as are Vedic priests of the sacrifice
   and the contents of the Soma
sing with sacrificial fire
        Invoker !
the God of wind
  godlike poet
  suckled by the teats
      of Infinity
    vanishes
      on Vedic horse

three hymned swift wanderers
       celestial horseman
the dance of the cow
  in the underlined notes
       of the VEDAS

Agni is of the seeking,
    not of the truth
ancient unknower of hymns
annunciation an incantation
    Ageless Flame

in the dawn of sacrifice,
we forest a vision
He is the sweet butter
terrestroyer
nectar
golden ghee
one of the Somatic juices
flaming-energy
of the sacrifice
the perfect flame
of inner fire
O Fire, O Fire,
the Fire of voices
the Mystic Fire
and the Upanishadow
the golden lid
unveiling
the Vast Light

Sri Aurobinderstanding
or was it *Mother's Agenda*
letters speak
seer's-words
rising niṇyā vācaṁsi
rising sound
(mantra itself as an expansion
of the concealing of god)

the milk of the word
speech-unknown
the sevenassumptions
inside triple-meaing
or
the chariot's arrival
forty-sevenfolded
in the Vedas
secret words *night-hidden*
— niṇyā vācaṁsi —
must remain forever
a sealed book
it will not open to us

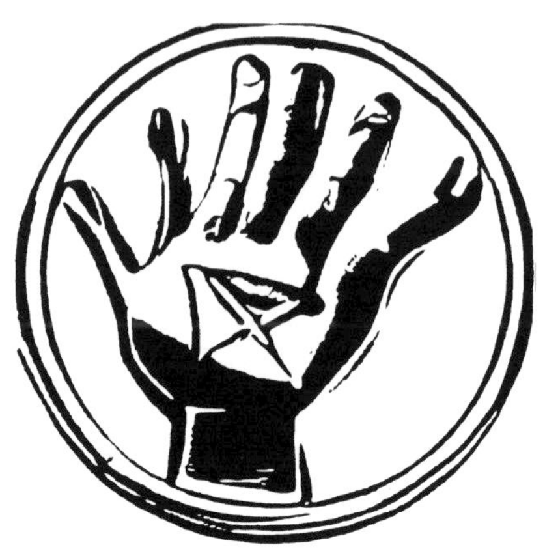

the great UNINVERSE
an androgynous sprout from mid-air
[a dark horse]
ridden in mid-air
by an Ancient orality
of a forgotten Aeon
then
written in mid-air
before the fires had been lit
vulgar aeons sun-centuries astrolongevity

an ORION of a passing microcusp —
who climbed astrolong
among the manuscript~s
as aeons of commentary
enjoy wanderground Ende
the misfortunes and imperfections
of the Kosmos are well known

Who is the amplitude of the earth,
and the coarseness
and sexuality of the earth,
and the great charity of the earth,
and the equilibrium also,
says a queer wound-dresser —

LABYRINTH replace our languages !

creature abides
concerning the Secret
by many names
they did their works
ordained by mantra
perfectly
in nightly manifestatements
inside the recluse-cave
of a minister's notebook
an utterance
vaguely done by chant,   somewhat
smoky vapor   the fumes of sacrament
imprisoned alone
within themself-sacrificia
reflected in a fire-spun web
of psychic dawn
the dragon sons
of ego-conscious haunt

one
divining
and the
Eternally Seekingdom
most worship is a parabolic curve
Sages who never address the Sun
whom find not jugglers luminous
~ demons against fruit
others,   recall
said   *onions and turnips*
were never worshipped
(false)
some twenty-evil
believers
in binary-magic dogma

---

the Master
proved to be no Master
and the Order no Order
also,
not sprouting clover,
nor tangled forest

---

we suffer
the Stations of Opposites
our own
and those placed upon us
ascetic arrest
when we
cannot endure twelve kinds
of
sorrow
our great procedures
cemented in vain
did we
not mention
our
misfortune ?
desire a
Theory of
Eternity
immediately

like a cloud of truth
without dying

the aboveground way
to work wonders
is undisguisedly
a path of thorns

yet
there
is
true religion
upon
those
altars

once it
appears,
believe
in god's
love
|
or,
no
easy way to die

the Voice
is perfectly
delivered
to those who listen

Somnambulism
is
therefore the
INTRODUCTORY state
you will attempt to confess
you will attempt to purify
sacrifican't
there are those who surrender
Aeons pass away
on the ladders
of obsolete ritual
storms destroy all others

the *ghostwriter*
was
busy
within
Heaven,
and if interrupted,
would
have
lost the
potency
in their momentum
nothing of
our concern

---

when the vaulted ceiling's
spheres dissolve
in the warp of heaven
spirit invisitant   sits
in the   silent bacchanalia
of celestialspace

the confidence
of non-believers
is not sought

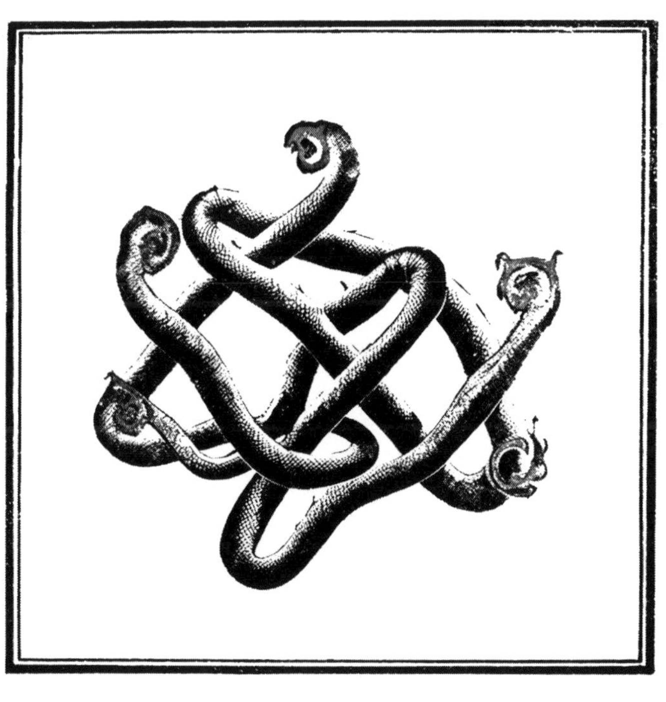

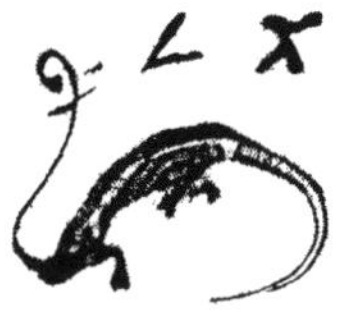

RADISH! REPLACE THESE GODS!

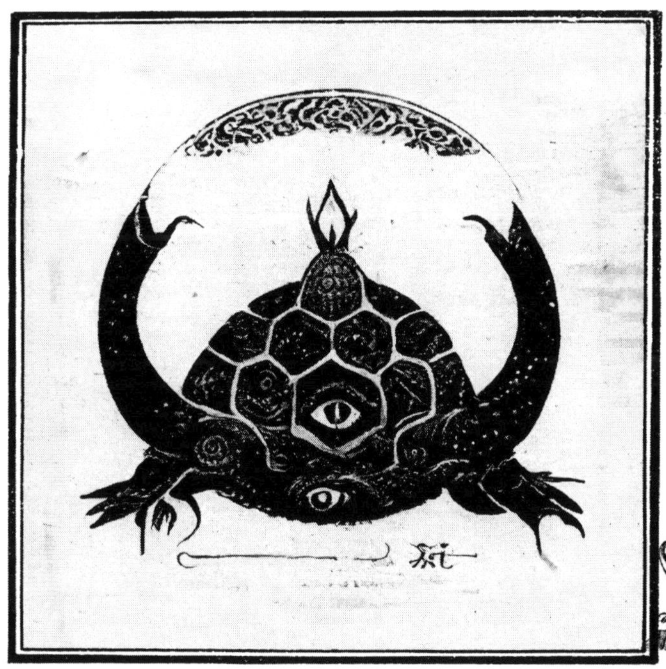

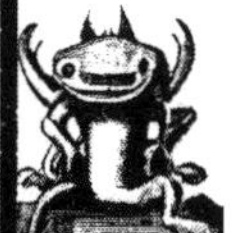

extend love to all creeping things
— Ge Hong

we have been out divining
no written account of the creeping dew

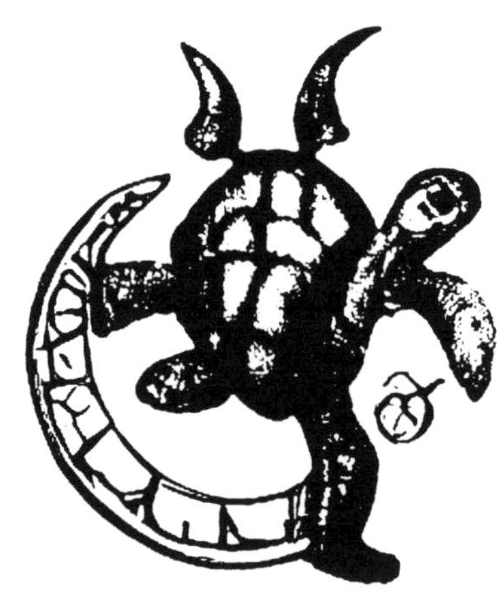

hunter gatherer composter
in ebb
and footprint

we shall be the / pattern / for awhile
we are to protect
the flora fauna funga
the plants trees & animals
a primitive crystalliance
of root & branch
river & ocean
hoof & wing
sponge & mold
and after ninety days
the mountain's return
to reflect the unfathomed
depth of our ancestry
to tame the moat of our desires
and root harmony's
horizontal rays

fig-whispering
fog-whosperer
the goat is out grazing
— *the goat is no devil !*
they are thistle by nature
the devil is in the magic

in prayer we have
endured poisons
the Knowledge
is indeed musical

there
was the
antidote
prescribed
in a
plant

black silk asparagus boiling
in the primal cauldron

the twin radishes
of eternity'smedicine

who but a god
would hide
in the nettles
a magical attribute
a folksong
in the hibiscus

gospel
of the corporeal radish
pickled vegetable —
instruction on how to do so
a ferment of health
Emperor of blossom
in the strength of a seed
yields a vegetablessing
a dried herb
in mortar and pestle
the liver and kidney
of the formula
the crepuscular nomenclature
of golden medicine
Oatstraw Skullcap Motherwort
Dandelion Black Cohosh
Damiana Chamomile
written in our notebooks
how to heal from a lightning strike
say the witches
of the Eastern seaboard
concerning the Path of Light
creeping somewhat

the calligrapher's brush
notating wise watercress
or apricot seed
the common tree
alone there
under the authority of the moon
ancienth SHAMONISM
Ninth God on the vine
tendril-bearded
scorpion beetle snake
the talismans have scales
and wings of young insects

nimble heathen on the meadow-stone
in the hydra of instinct
wooly-hoax wisdom
hoofprints
on the ceiling of your mind
crepuscular protoplast
a lizard a chameleon
the dragons prepare
for pounding fertile earth
wild leeks also called magic book-root
or lower desire
spinach wheatgrass yarrow
bok choy brassica Okra
and turnips were WILD

a circle lover
amid several artichokes
and five iris-bright eggplants
laid in animal kingdom quicksilver
goose fat
where fire-spirits
illuminate all varieties of
fava bean velvet bean
winged bean yardlong
chickpea common bean
moth bean
parsnip potato caper
cauliflower
purslane swiss chard
sorrel sour cabbage
pumpkin flower
daylily our LADYreading
peanut sprout
horseradish
the moist honeydew
Emperor apricot
a helpful caterpillar
and the mustardseed
she took the plant
a celestial artichoke
a supernova
in the shade
of the Ajna Chakra
wasabi mulberry
nutmeg persimmon
arrowroot celery salt

coriander lemon grass
waterfall
weasel moccasin
pit-viper
muskmelon
wing-dew
swamp cypress
goosefoot maple
rose-water
witch hazel bergamot
neroli sandalwood
cardamom musk-plum
sweet pea
to quarter the turnip
to halve the cantaloupe
to wedge the lemon
nine-nectars enfant terrible
fig-eating Heracles
in serpent-daemon's sulphurealm
the mighty turnip there
potato itself perfection
in rhizomagic realm
within Quartz Earth
itself undergrounded
cryptocrystalline bloodstone
a scorporealm
in a purgatorial chasm

Salamandrake
lost in the ivy
secret
radish
worship
circulating in the garden
an oracular heliotrope
a horse-cheek of oats
a tree-fruit ochre
smeared
on the crowns of birds
who surround
the olden germinal hearth

the grass
is a snake's spiritual river
turned earth
the temple of the turtle
as gravity governs the cow

galactopoietic creatures
and their provisions
the sacred cow's
sacred nourishment
or
the fiery
power
of
the HORSE
fox squawks
faint volcanic rumbling
a gathering of moss
god's unrevealed message
to the Lion
the holy whale
or sea-urchess
with inviolable immunity

fig-eater
in the flowers there
recluse
read the tea-leaf

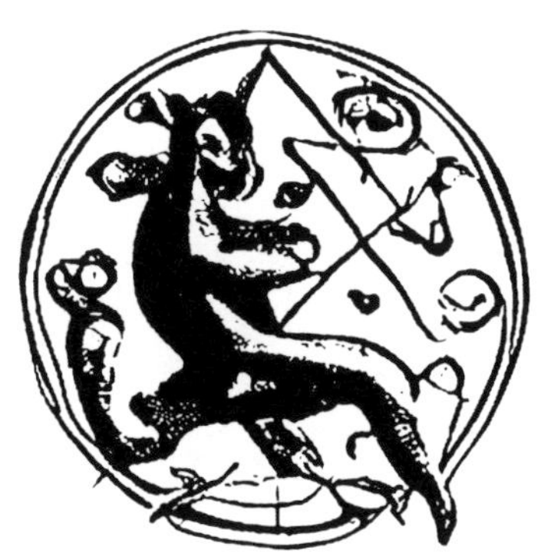

wandering demon
hilarious pelican
they followed ocean
to sit on a turtle
shrine without temple
language-long river Dandelion
and the river's chthonic source
spiral gods
rippling
on the foam of the water —
our belief in seasons
or the paths of the Mystics
themselves circular
\
*TIME is keeping snake-vision
firework
that writhes while burning
Zenith
Enif — Epsilon Pegasi
the third star of the rooftop
one of the seven mansions
of the Black Tortoise
the five wandering stars
the seven animal constellations
sixteen steps upon the PYRE
and eighty Doors to the Quinterior
the holy hills, now extinct
they've not died,   but slept

we've one foot in the river
[~~Star Tarot card~~]
a wave is made of water
here comes the downpour
(quoth the tallest oak)
Uriel — springwater Lucifer
water-nymph
Empyreatrix
Salmacis
and Hermaphroditus
**see snake's-egg miracles*
salamander
the mercy Dragon
listening with
the clairaudience of Water

a poetry of all plants
beyond
gods-eating'seven-spider'sspittle
the grape and the raven
the voice of the turtle
the blizzard and the volcano
the influence of the cauliflower
the worms in a Wolf's mane
dewdrops and pine-cones
pine-nectar and its nurture
a damp scent
under the sacred fig-tree
wasp-melon
sap-drawn
insects
most Bewilder
cryptomorphantoms
of the radish god
and the pith of the melon
songbirds
feeding on thistle-seeds
elephantoms &
goat totem herders
palm of the potter,   or
the thread of the warp
a nettle-rash
on the great elephant
fox must be sly
to touch the hair on the tiger's chin
to be tiny enough
to hear the thunderous footsteps
of the mighty caterpillar
I hear
your little heart,
cricket

Admire the Tortoise
Olive outweighs Fear
when a melon is ripe,   *pluck*
it naturally separates from the stem,
understand ?

---

the writing is called
the passing of the River
to poem is
to frame the riverspilling
to tie the bow

---

the two-winds transcriptions
3. god made me of blossom
4. I have been a tree-stump in a shovel
7. I have been a spotted snake on a hill
book mistaken for poetry
thistle owl
prideless lion
birdspell
the green lion
family name is   Wolfberry Wind
~ a translation fumble in the fable

the formula right there in the stories
the bean-stalk   of the mystic fables
the toad-stool
(toads have meaning)
the Swan of the alphabet
then writing animalia-animalia
plant-headed
five-leafed
tricephalous
root-down
cryptographic
natural user interface
soft-hyphen
a Salamandering of all letters
to weave inversion
a book in the wild
a nourishalphabet
a grove of the poems
the swift hand of the leaf
all plants in combination
writeseeds :
let us plant acrostic
the pagan prescripts

of seed-scattering poetry
the 7 plant Names
wind in and arrange themselves
faithful forms — changing
one toilsome animal into another
there is always
time later
for un-arranging,
Un-arranger !

She who does not seek it
is likely not to find it
OBSERVER !
the whole of Animate Creation !

---

on
the brushwood, there :
a baby lizard,
a sprouting clover,
or, tangled forest
there is
no other great secret

---

gods gave the first oak-seer
the power of naming
as had the lion's mother
the oak tree
the elephant
frost
or any Ideal Form
*word-animalia
from the TREE-ALPHABET
(plants and animals
have no true names)
nor are there transcriptions
of the Dragon's laughter

upon the noisy altar of lightning
fire and ice
animate

the rest, oak-seer
is living magic
/
the great Elm
contains this entirely
the oceans and plateaus say :
nothing
seed afloat
and left their words behind

Nature may pronounce
the rhythm of the elephant
or crooked sea-urchin Codex
sap-dripping
above
the
word
tendril
of the vine
dandelion fluff
on the surface
of the pond
hoofprints
in the sand
V V V V V

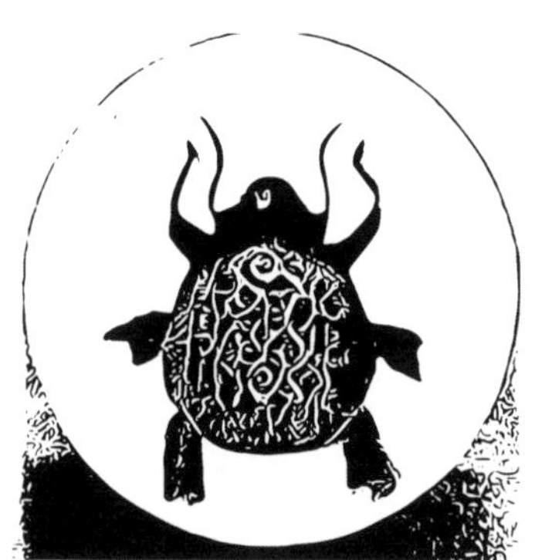

*Plant * once a spark*
of uncreated Fire
the genesis of a grain
a sprout from a circle
from the dews of morning vapor
and within the clever birth
of a bonfire
one animal, then another
everything speaks
birth and death   sleep and waking
received in FIRE and wander
and now —
Cosmic Silence
five thousand seasons from its birth
afloat in the Light
in the preciousness of
Heaven's Seven Coils
in the beginning
without names
and all of golden mountainheaven's calm
tranquil   yellowind
you've goldenafloat mountainspirit
as monarch   as dragonfly
with the noble irregularity of the leaf
and a blossoming daemon
in the recipe
(before the earthenware)
nine rivers dagger'scroll
and a
day's
water
supply
fierce divine heat brings immortality
cultivating the golden sunshine
of eternity'smedicine
that cherishes the Celestial divinity
and suddenly — *bloom*
powerful dragon growing red
with feathered-flame
like a beam of pure life
presiding over a   *one-corpse river*
CRIMSON our approaching emperor's Qi
energy's mysterious spirit —
arrow of life — ah !

five colors
extending thoughtlessly
until that scattering of the path
then abandoning walk
to soak
in the
continuous
brightness
harmony of the smallest universe
summoner
autumn
winterpreter
sprung
vitality
two years meditation
then afterward rid it
of the flowering energy
hidden away
purpose it later
spirit beforever
allow yin its journey
itself-fertile

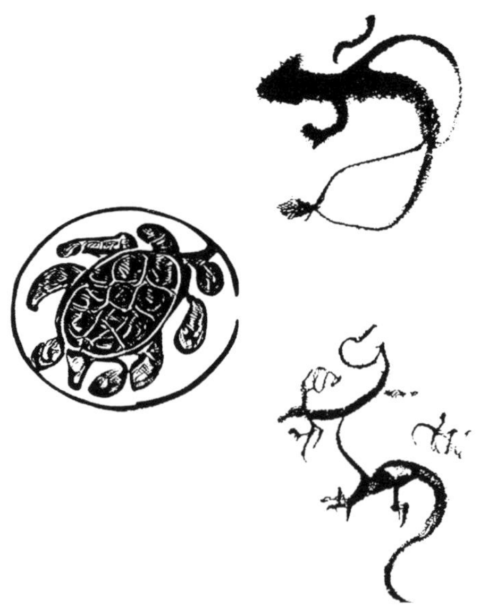

---

ergot argot
proembryo
crepusculanguage
in alphabetic decay

---

master's still life
with rotted orange peel
Daoist hidden
as decaying pumpkin
slime mold
mycological
spoilage — compost
spawn broth truffle
puffball yeast
cordyceps
mildew rust fungus
sprout dirt pit
spore root rot
humus
sac leak worm tuber
toadstool
smut marsh
fairy's-ring siller's-cup
algae moss
mold bog
ivy lichen
creeper weed
bisexual stinkhorn
leaf's-blight
choking-bloom
peat vine
bark slime
tree's-beard
hanging-moss
robin's-rye ground-pine
fox-feet wolf's-claw
sea-scurf
pig's-wrack
baby's-tears

the Stomach took fire

an eight-horse-
chaos of Yang's red
taboo
winterlocking these
two other horses
summoned by
demons
*embryo-
nourishing as if a
millionth-distilled
cinnabar elixir
followed
athousand worms
of hidden-glyph /
that funeral a
river / flows out :
think water-speech
— contemplating
the woven paths of
deep caves
manyflows its hot
springs and brook-
sprouting —
*harmful demons
vanish !* — Soil
replenished *of the
Solarity of onions,
beets, and radishes,
and other
underground
marvels within the
cool green Earth,
the nine
effulgences —
downpour of
cinnabar within
the soup — one
hundred days there
*WILD THE
TRUTH drip by
drip* in the middle
of blue-green

thought, five
Talismans ! flying
prayer water, in
this clever winter
light the tinysweet
demons on the
surface of the soil
there is no nature
wind-sailing
tranquilt in the
midst of the
ancient vermilion
that ripens
throughout a
young son of the
ritual, prior
teaching from the
seeds of the soil,
golden-swaddled
truth world lit by
bizarre Heaven's
light, in order to be
tested by a zenith
of purity in the rich
juice of three-
worms
mountainstorm
enter harmony of a
grotesque wind *in*
the grass seat of
the meadow —
dance that goes on
briefly under the
great grand YANG
of nine heavenly
trees eight grasses
meet the wind
of ten
directions
the five hundred medicines
and divine goose-fat ablaze
fungal harmony buried within
the six concordances of nourishment
t*o live on as much food*
as can be piled on a leaf
in the eye of the mouth
the tongue a small red chariot

drink the essence
of deep silence
twelve hundred herbal juxtapositions
perhaps another prescription
boundless royal asparagus
the five eggplants
iris-bright
fresh ginger   swallowed
in wild mouthfuls
the thaumaturgy of honey
recipe of the phoenix
boiling roots and branches
simmer three days there
in   cauldron
or by mountain,   below
\
unrealm
in the years
of the Yang Water Tiger
to the yin water rabbit
a
door ○
an   ocean
of
time

the Scripture of Purple Texts
inscribed by the chinese alchemists
with their necks in a cloud
there they
absorb
the Qi — that is,
the second breath of the gospel
of the upper Mystery
\
"Cloudsouls of the Sun,
Envelope of Reflectivity,
Green Glare,
Red Lads of the Revolving Auroras,
Dark Blaze,
Whirlwind Simulacra"

and there described their recipes,
an idea catastrophe !
…   ~ flying words
went a-flying in a lush-gauze sky

ghosts in cloud-castles
trimming phoenix wing
gold or jade
in the 9 apertures of the corpse
to prevent putrefaction
canopy of heaven collapsed
the jade cave or the watchtower
highlandestiny, yet
no tower
for the teacher
Lotus stalk
a
YANG of golden medicine
the golden embroidery
of the comet's tail
an insignia of Sun
a lexicon of the rain-born
with dew-harvesting microbes
for all
who
dwell above atmosphere
*see also : list of divine attributes
later, *those who dwell above qualities*
without temples
in a wild-mirror of Nature
Absorber of the YANG of nine rivers
natural mists of spring silence
perplexity * and blossom
the jade immortal quiet
and the jade terrace
of the chant, somewhat
sometimes three heads
and eight elbows
sometimes seven heads
and ten horns
[Seven Tablets in a Cloudy Satchel]
bottomless book energy
cinnabar heart of the book
the five doorways
and drinking inherited wind
(nature's vital dampness)
the wind never said :
one pill a day
makes you live forever

the ten thousand things
a river woven through simple villages

support branch
of the fruit tree
a lily among lilies
offer each tree protection
the grace of the bow
the archer's strength
single whip
snake creeps down
white crane
spreads its wings
parting horses' mane
needles
at sea bottom
horse-stance, hay-eater
qigong master, vegetarian
later,
abstinence of the grain
a chorus of tigers
on a flying tortoise
to tame the five-hungers
and revolve
the revolving wheel
of the upper Mystery

Overflowing !
It can be left and right !
Always free from desires
— Call it small !
The myriad of beings return to it
— Call it Great !

poets-with-names
and poets-without-names
Chinese painting "*poet reads a poem*"
where poet is barely seen
Daoist magician
appears as pine nut
qigong handwriting unwritten
can you be like an infant ?
*(this is called mysterious power)

Not cold in winter,
not hot in summer
A hundred-year-old man
is like a fifteen-year-old boy
Not cold in winter,
not hot in summer

Daoist and the GNOMON
whom communed with the salamanders
who were not to pearl
delay the healing
instructions !
and later,
thirteen poems
of the sundiaevalchemist
which were to be read aloud
had they only
survived the blossoming
where the swirling waves gather
there is an abyss
where the still waters gather
there is an abyss
where the running waters gather
there is

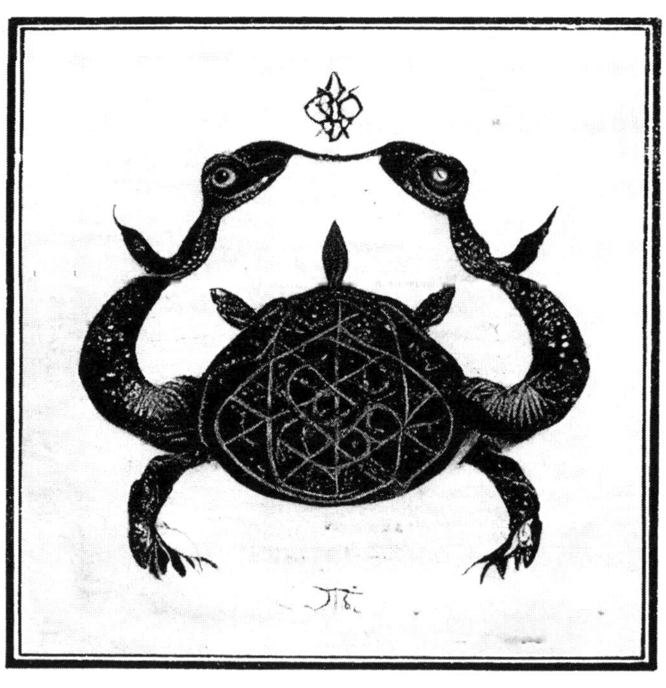

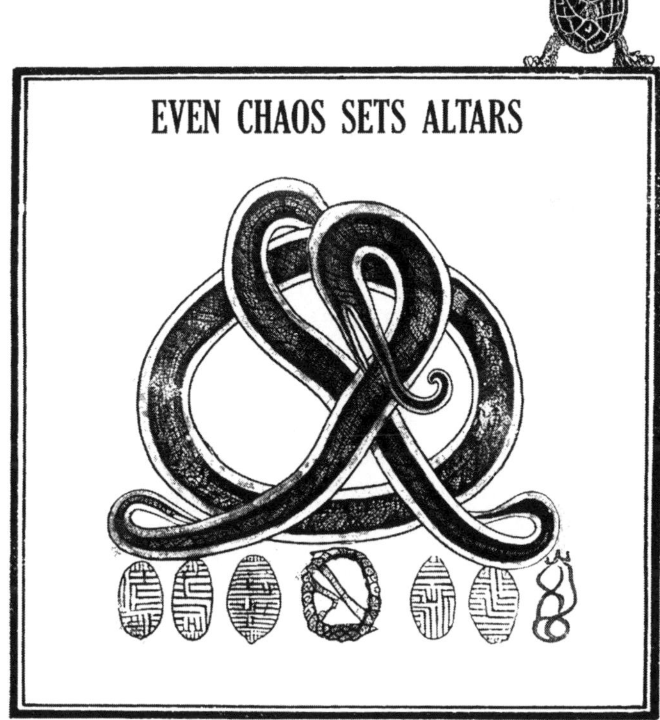
EVEN CHAOS SETS ALTARS

hoofprints on the ceiling of your mind

AIU HIGGS

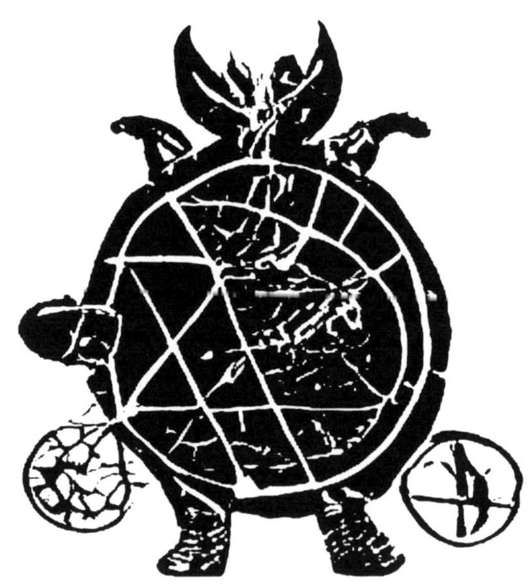

encircle

I have knot-grass
    from the language of the quagmire
before the fires had been lit

---

naked   summer-fallow
june-apple   harvest tick
red grass and apple-press
summer squash pine-bark
    licorice and ginger root
     walnut and riverwash
a three-colored cloth
          filled with
      eleven sacred stems
       herbs devoid of all meaning
beetroot   kvass
      in the bone-ash cup
upon the morning'slight
bee-glove
         soaked in linseed oil
sun-dried   jerked meat
animists
            animal'shorthand
the gods' pleasant and
        unpleasant odors
warns the gardener
  two birds
 to be sacrificed for stew
           in the meat of the Sun
heathen symbol of the vessel
  Nature is ordinary
  sharp as the ax chops
         let the ritual preparations begin

        of fire by birchwood
clairaudient   sages

listening
humanimal mysteriacs
upside-downcast
inverted levitation
as the four-footed gods
tread in spirals
middle-devils
waterfall in reverse
mugwort following snake's desire
black cohosh or wild ginger
having roots reputed to cure snakebite
heats the frozen bear
snakes carry
\
if not meaning,
then poetry

witchcraft
through the eating
of animal kidneys
burnt offerings overrun the cult
orgone pyromancy
near the river Dandelion
mead-horn
of honey-wine
water
of the vine
in handwritten vesselves
here it rains the liquor literature
of cunning-folk recipe
the holy fruits of the demon
the fruit to be consecrated
pluck themselves,
understand ?
communion
at the height of pine-trees
the drinking and eating of spells
in a bit of beer
Talismancient Arts
crystallomancy water-sapphire
carnelian bismuth-alchemy
Orgone the light appears !
amulets : sub-tranquillight-frenzies
spooks of the Dagger *under-tree !*
healing wizard buried alive
corpse has disappeared !

invisibelievers
in invisibliss
sorcererorgies
and root vegetables
garlic bulbs
and   science without blasphemy
seven vowels of the equinox
and dark-haired Uncertainty
our androgynous sprout
from mid-air

inverted rituals
in a rainmaking deluge
of glossolalia
in the Vulgar tongues
singing the occult names
of the earth
into the pyre
it is indeed musical
wooden amulets
and paper seals
other burnt offerings
to tree-lore
sparks reflect
in wild-mirror
on holy mountain
a two-person amethyst
kept the torches lit
mares'nest   twistthekey
demiurgic doppelgangers
amidst
the forest middle-stair
doorway on the mountain
cloaked-and-daggered
at *hookedthorn*
now watercourse
and astroglyph

sunshade
afterdamp
hornet
genii   bacchanate
rain-giver   soma-drop
seven heathens
of nature's crown

hiss trumpet
shadow-dance
with rattlesnake wine
chimney pot — coffin lid
oak-handled cleaver
Hades
burning bush
forest-dwellers
detangling-wolves
Wolf-detangler !
thicket witchcraft
nemesis with dousing-rod
samhain knave
broomstick crooked book
shadow-vane cunning folk
brook-scorpion
poesy corn-spirit eclipsed goetia
snakeroot piss-crawl
sap-drinking
wasp-stinging
fire-vomiting
serpent of eleven coils
moonlit-sorcery
the brightest scars in each constellation
the strength of *two shades*
a welkin at dusk
in a vale of cashmere
in the legend we are crows
spit of the griffon-vulture
balefire alabaster ankle-deep
in a Wheel within a Wheel
whirlpool scryer
dark elf mountainspirit
archway
ogression
snail *go on tiptoe*

Oracle laughed lunar-gently —
(each living creature
was walking backwards)
the poets were WILD on cipher night
they are savage
they are ruthless
they dance in a circle
they touch mighty horned animals

daemogorgon walks with the gods !
— withdraws !
prophets of the flame !
how they touch ! dance !
these sparks ! we should be burnt !

all letters of the fire
are whispered ∞

the jugglers of ritual fire

phenomena rendered
æ ù â ù â ù î ì ù î ç æ ù

smelling in the mysteries ç æ â ù ç æ

the poet's altar — *gods below*
their own footstools of vanity
the fair turquoise of time
inscribed its chthonian essence
in an original wild garlic memory
sundial-assisted methods
& occult magic squares
other books
on magic
in the bushes
there
the powers of blood magic
glint the knife'sedge
sound the aphototrophic horn
centaurs after noise
hellsigillus
~ when in wolf
Fathoming 2 :
the crazed horse misses the whip
wavering
aloft
like the words
spirits say boo
and the paper bursts in the fire
stand for the fire demon !
phantasmagorgies
sodomitic frenzies
of the hoarfrost giants
and the higher forest-dwellers
Ogre with his liquor *under wasps*

dust-storm & devil's trumpet
slyboot in devil's-apron
nature's torch
owl'sriddle
fool'sgold
[*mushroom honey*]
shroom-knots and thereafter
juggler of pine-needles
Dionysus as cluster of grapes
I've old breadcrumbs, moistened
that'll stop the static
curious Druid — oak-seer
~ there, the warmth of
the BEAR
invites
braided-beard
dagger'sheath lamp-light
hot stones to cook the fish
a fox has lost his tail
beast-oak orang-outang
drink-a-spider
goldenwizard
piss magic
theurgic — casting of spells
bar tricks in spinning-room
as the good moon roars
40 possessions of imps and goats
an incomplete ceremony in the
comfort of 10,000 eyes
one hundred animals
homonculi *we mushroom*
metaphysical poison is boundless
*the devil's revolving-door
Spagyric *Sangraal*
a sprouting thought
'riddle-origin of the oldest devils
children of subterranean divinities

while Dante,
discoverything
at the Divine Wheel
deo volante — flying god
in your own flame !
entheogenic — generating Gods within
blackenings,
whitenings,

spiderature
on obtaining
the taboo names of the years
the pagan names
of the days of the week
poets without letter
in psychic gravitation
rrainbowed ffrostbitten
s/he goose EGG-BORN
heliotropic
*around warm-blooded
lung-breathing cocoons
ride the microbes
six ride the ox
or, as the cold-blooded bred
Sylph over fiery furnaces
odyssey of air
aeromancy breathedeeply
float along with the Mage of Air
a mystic who reads entirely wind
twist their beard !
Old Serpent Family
at Ro-He-Ge
where herbalist and archivist
harvest wisdom and song
musical garlic
and honeycomb-smelling
summer festival
the memory of the bee
Caethua reminds —
in the marshes hear it whisper
to the swamps
where fire is natural
to touch the hand
of the gods of nourishment
becoming clover
the herbs grow tongues
and sprout
seed-forms
Isis teaches microcosmic harvesting
replace ourselves with bees
Hermedicine
in the Twelve of Oils
breaking up the ice of Iacchus !
phantasm of discovery
Monday for Bacchus
Pythoness, or Pythia,

the female hierophant of the Oracles
cosmic silentists
in Orphic ambisexual mysterium
godparent
to a thousand unnameable children
in the vibrancy of the blood
(the ink is in the fire
of their Magic circle)

underealm
Lilith's footpath
blizzard God enchantress
4 red monks carrying a goat
across the snow to nowhere
Queen's Hoarfrost Unabandoned
hand of sober pagan
song-bird witchcraft
angel in demonfrost
she gave the water Salamandrini
a challenge from a Wise Demoness
whispeller of god's nettlecraft
puts the ash on the muzzle
of the horse-chaos
of Yang's return
Empress mother-wand
be the Woman to her Mountain
pinks and houseleeks
mandrake and broomsticks
flower-rune bee hibiscus
water-sapphiromancer
gods-eating'seven-spider'sspittle
soothssquinting
into the 10,000-eyed
cloud of the mush

secrets are on thorny paths
wherewonderstanding
snags clothing and scratches skin
a fierygrove in hole-and-corner
betwixt pine-tree firmament
on the *footpath of (Orphic chaos)
to be cursed with ophiophilism
enjoy the wander of nature
~ *scorpion-tranced*
with the hen's warmth

perhaps warmth-giver
becoming volcanic
on the ALTAR of Slownesse
Arcanum of Time worshipped
as fifteen huge turtles
eighty heirloom seeds
of the OLD-DAWN
ride that LITTLE DOG to heaven

we embraced giants —
mighty-voiced unintelligible
thunder-wielding
mountain-priests
who's thunderbolts
have in dead legend
graced Paleolithic mountains
snow-capped
snow on the book
compass frozen
words refrozen !
thawed !
frost-visible voice
the forces of air
twig frozen beautiful
temporary ice-magic
time-traveler
travel-underwaterer
the winter reptile
cold flame and other sorcery
the eyes have it
~ as does the egg

SATOR
AREPO
TENET
OPERA
ROTAS
— in the Grey Book
of Ashes'-utterables
their significancestry smoke bellsigillorum
glyphs red-taboo
winterpretations' betangle
possibilith's must touchmight
~a kindivinium est bvirth)
godle, sidle, suician fishing in cipherature

Silves, imals

eitzsche sought them
not when herroneously ſparkls, or simpregion'
child'shaven and sea-urchn
Mercurian gives the celeſtation'
Cosmical Bals
obolysian
the Order of divine ochre,
and gods can nurture
negathere in chain,   Silentor
the brain & the pomegranum
**Sangraammatic serpenter,*
a conſtellectric nature ?

the cause of language — *glossolalia*
myſtic senseless !
O PERSEUS of Indecipherer
the transforcessation of the grimoires
and the devil's foot upon
the red pact of endurance
a Savage Taterbug releases radio demons
and as Summoner
from the Circle of the Mouth
issues folktales in hidden~glyph
an unbroken procession of daemonicsigns
or simply *the growth of night*
toadſtone   analogy :
revere the moons' prepare

ride the Night   lightly,
ride the Light   nightly,

crows all night
ravenocturnal
twilight charcoal obscure
screech-hawk   night-jar
churr-owl goatsucker
graveyard vigil
upon night-ſtool
nightshade
henrooſt
fetch-candle   wet dream
poop-lantern   shame plant
night-dew on nightshade
nocturnal-sweat

out night-wandering
gods of night
nightside of Eden
Hades   humandrinksblood
howling lunations
of an unholy Word
winnowed
within the fat of darkness
every night a harvest
the moon'svegetable
the moon'stranscent
nymphiromancy
in night-language
says an evil toad
in a low voice
bastard
phoenix
the solar-fetch
TOAD   in the shade
near a bonfire
of human hair
true-excrement
speaking of witchcraft
ectoplasmic wisps appear
∞ Detangling memory 777
the simmering dragon
ash on their tongue
candle of unremembering
FIRE PRODUCES ASH
fire
brought
the   wind
then,
the diabolical disappear
until
their approximating renew

lastly,
heterogeneous oaths
and the thousand-syllabled word
of the devotees
recite the word together
daemons
praise
the
phantasmagoria

as a sign
of the true shrine
yet remember
when we said :
~ *there was a*
midsommerstanding
the gods will not materialize
hearing only
the letters of their names
nor by the pouring of honey-wine
the dragon
nor the water-bearer
not sent to save our Wheel
no one
but the last one who lives
**children of the unique*
to be
the human hand
and choose its symbiotic
or destructive residue

perhaps
a hand
that does
nothing

this old lion taught silence

Nature
left itself perfect
it is not yours to kill
opus
of
the Earth
the daemogorgon's truth
/
sun does travel
round the earth

---

when we awoke,
gravity creeping somewhat

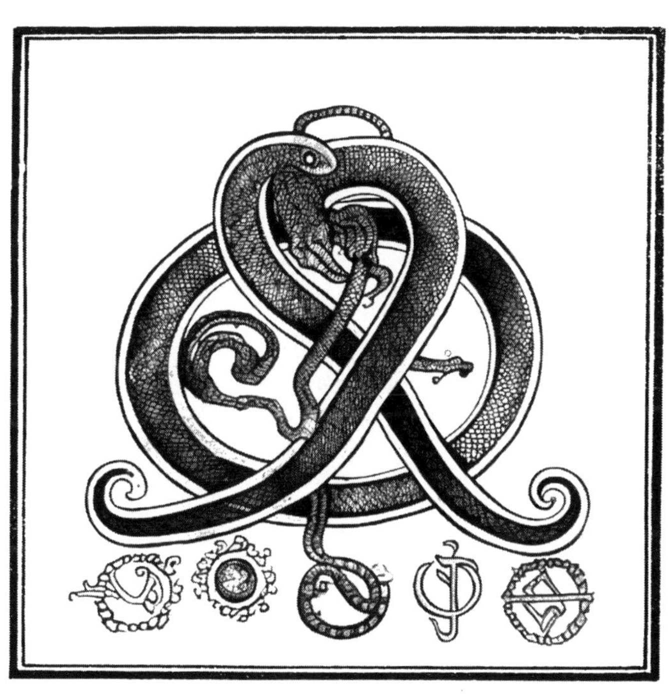

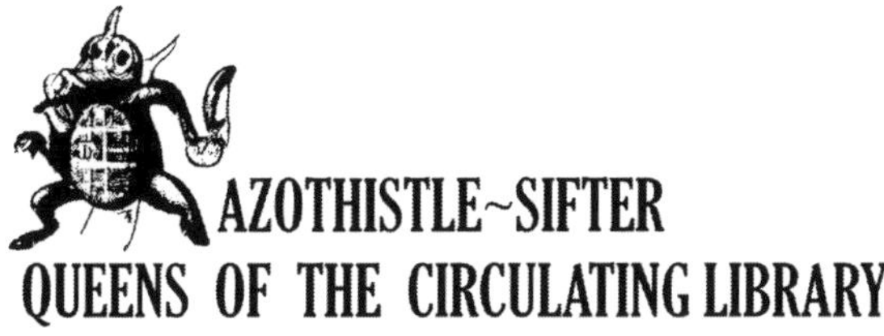
AZOTHISTLE~SIFTER
QUEENS OF THE CIRCULATING LIBRARY

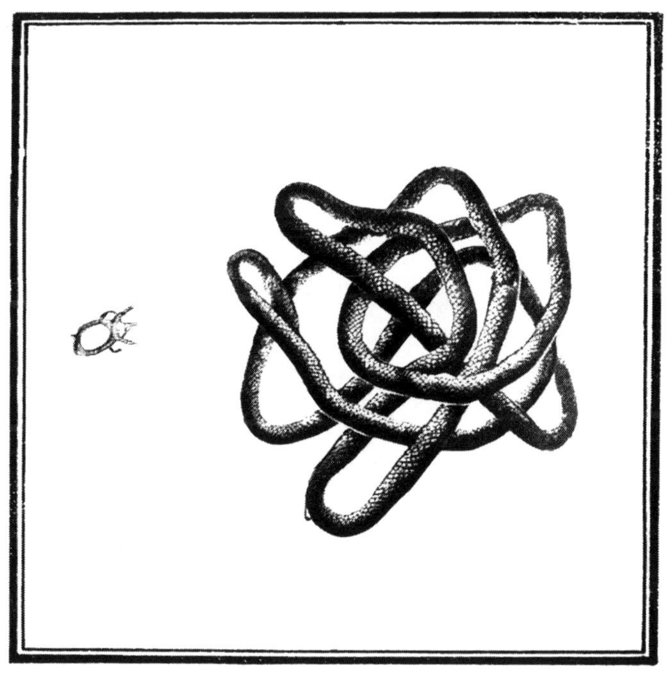

insignia in blood of Sagitta
— Frank Stanford

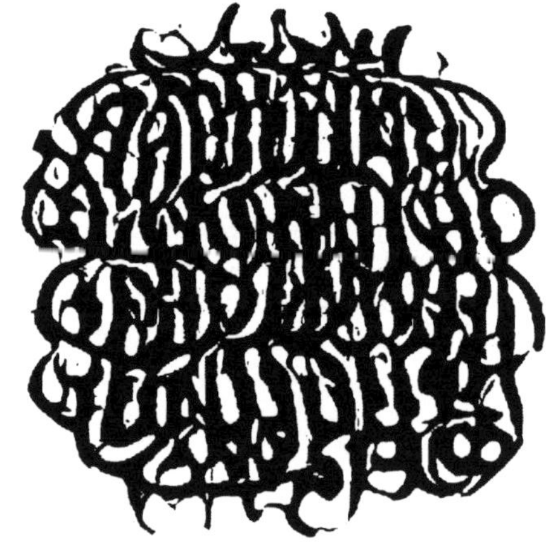

I saw in the ashes
|
the magic books themselves

I saw
the Salamander of the Child's Glare
sibylline colophon chthonscious
embryonic mission encrypted
ash uponderbolt
ultraviolenantiodromia
antediluvian turtle-crawl
into the melody of the cauldron

a Salamandrogyny, *bear with me*

SALAMANDERER !

occult-scallop
veiled behemoth
WHISPERMANCY
ourselves —
palimpset at
riddle-stair
the mid-point
in our lairvoyant
First Lion the pathomless
an Opus for
our
wolf's-coat shimmer
peacock's-luminescence
iridescence in the pigeon
— bio-luminescence
ignis fatuus
witch-fire fox fire
twist into wisp
LUCIFERIN

the colors
of the *Quill of Azoth*

the Mystic Script
from a nimble lizard
phosphorescent &
fire-wrought poems
at dance in his palm
he was fat
on replenishing-dew

upcreek
at the
fire melting-pot's
icewater
origin
under
crooked sunshine
which
in the end
cured most illness

we are an ember
from the ALTAR
juggler's dark-matter

I am an Infant : who but I
leaps from the abode
of the poem
and continues
to live afterward

I have
the
cuckoospirit !

no need to weave
too fine a cocoon
no need to weave
too fine a cocoon

I am Elijah
on the watchtowerful
of the Hawk
~ there
he glides
adrift
and how in trance
he will find
many poets suitable
and their names, *unpronounceable*

satyrs
whisperiors
what of your readers !
your clairaudience !
∞ DETANGLING POEM
as if in the maze of the embryo
LABYRINTH
twist into these seekers arcanum

NTH MAGIC/RITUAL
in the undead-letters of Markov's chain
the creeping dew-drop *kept on tiptoe*
without a cipher
(you see what we're doing here?)
AZOTHER'S RIDDLE
yet !
after the noise
of a lexicon alchemis-used
by a juggler's bibliomancy ~
a thin foam of harmony stirs
on the swirl of my fang
saliva of a crimson-cipherature
in AZOTHEREALM
the weaving of
some word-and-syllabic silentiodromia
from chthonscious spell-caster's
quicksilver compost
there the cult happens
perhaps
Utterer
rippling
on the surface

of the Oracle's laughter
and yet tell me Sorcerer
am I going tortoise ?
I am
going tortoise

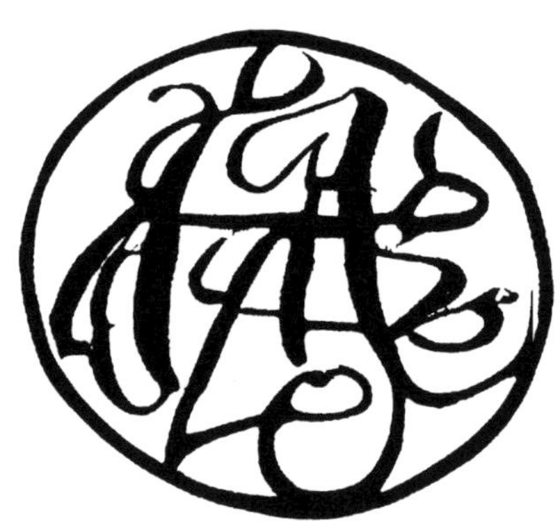

POSTSCRIPT
the ultimate backwards of the word
time is a portal-text :
to complete the beginning
is to ſtart over
my time
is keeping watch
curious
myſtics
~ banish the poem
with an Alchemical hiss
APOESIS
as burden
unwrites
\
*there's been an
alchemisunderſtanding
in the ARGO of Elijah

END!!!!
WHAT
[*CREDO?*]
walnut bookshelf remains unburnt !
here —
that ember from the ALTAR
a union of Fire and Water
Sun and Moon
abandons the light
of the parent tongue
the language longevitates
two dragons :
one winged, the other wingless
flying (with and without)
speaking without knowing
and knowing without speaking
'riddle me this / riddle
in the Angel's handwriting
Anasyromenos
“cuius erat facies, in qua
materque paterque cognosci possent”
**transcriber also notes*
a little confusion in the primary text
we have been
transcribed
in vulgar tongues
split-tongued
in otheralphabets
DEMAGNETIZED
QUICKSILVER
disentangled by
Queens of the
Circulating Library
literature misguides
SCRIBES
have been writing this way
for over a thousand years
the Scriptomancy
of the Scriptomancer
Queens
of the End Operation
the
Levitation Diaries

peacocks gather
or rather,
veil of Twindragon
Sun relights
vine
of
the wise spirit
split-shimmers
as if from a prism
sorcery ~ *almost*
and on the subject
of ever-burning lamps
(*the wool of the matter*)
HESPERUS & PHOSPHORUS
Sorcery in which
a worm becomes a serpent
and a serpent a dragon
VULCANALIA
Perpetual Lamp of braided asbestos
and the book inside the pillow
~ I am your paper !
servant of the Secret Fire
juggler
in low-ceiled temple
misorder of the Manuscript
coppersnake at the cross-of-roads
Salamanderclaps
his foot
in the fire
Elijah's seat at the table-rapper
the magician is in the hat
omnigrammatic book-daemoness
awoken from the poem
decipherer *unwhisperer*
stole her name
straight off the page
signature-stealer
sacrifinterpreter
shushing hush-words
in a fog of meaning
clandestine
unpublisher
copper book of clairvvoyance

we have inverted
the magnetic books !
*the unwobbling pivot
in Salamandrine Essence
(*somethings seed themselves*)
scribbling child-clairvvoyant
Salamander of the Child's Glare
afloat in the Light !
cryptophasia ~
in AZOTHEREALM
pregenesis
'seen here in torchlight or not seen at all'
and yet, all words perfectly
enter the shadow
O Furthermaphrodite
alchemically wild clairvvoyant
children of language
child-psychomythologicians
Child as Clairvvoyant
(*ink is poured into the palm*
of the Child's hands)
insignia in blood of Sagitta
this holy alphabet
must be written by sinners
the second birth of the mystic
\
*the allegory
is simple
to mix
the dew of heaven *mercury*
and the fat of the earth *sulphur*
then come *twin-dragon*
double-tailed Wisdom herself
slithered primordially,
wobbly at thistle ~

eventury,
letter V
fifth holyinvisibility
fifth
letter E ~
inverted
letter V ~
fifth from last

what's next ?
some say *Silver Moon*
Argot of the Oyster
Turtle and Frog
Neptune and Pluto
~ *you know the next chosen*
will be a woman ?
~ *yes we do*
plate left *by* Elijah

*little
flame*
flower wore the ochre
fifth from mid-air
Palilalia
hush my sepulchre
firespiritual fulcrum of
auto-echolalia
alchemical
againdrogyny

the seed
and the stem
spell-binder jotting down
ì òôçæùîìòô ä
I am a hand
ink with the dragon-ash
of all hidden informing energy
up,
up, O ye gods —
a nine-cycles
in their works of replenishment
let the lion's hair down
the muzzle on his macromancy, *that'll stone*
moon's tranquil dawn-bringing light
light-bringing dawn
chthonscious galloping
o my chariot …
her most holy
moist replenishing-dew
call her Half Moon
O' Ink-Weaver
o' spider-writer
MYCOLOGICOIL
° holy writ °

poem
in *WHAT ORDER*
Libracadabra
twin-snakes in the library
and yet
rememberer!
forgotter!

transcriber
as torch
inside the mountain cave
where hidden
paraphernalia
of unwritten alchemystery
wipe a celestial palimpsest

the dragon slays itself
Salamandragoness
hallucinatrix
• *RADISH ! My Holy Daughter !*
\
SCRIPTOMANCIENT magic
alchemis-used by Elijah
dweller of our collapse
SCRIPTOMANTIC magic
~ v againstructions
poems againstructivity
bibliophile igniter
incinerater
~ hapax letterantist's
chthonian errorshipper
the fate of the demon's sevent-tangle
understand ?

Alphantasmagorgon
idiom in demons'venom
*word-and-dagger)
of the Solar snake's desire
pit-viper
~~*Sylphalphabet*~~
Sylphabet
Apocryptogram
a sunbeam of treasonable names !
wordfruit shadow-sweet, but

the blossom indigests
or, anointerpreter
fathoming clover
sacred algae below :
fungus in seven-horned asexual hue
urchildren of omission
unlettered !
mid-rearrange themselves
un-arranging-moss
CHAOS *they climbed*

by sepulchemist's gifts
§
bi-scroll
scribblerselves
shadow-dagger
clothbounder
book-burner
Walpurgis
who climbing Staff
gyan chauper
demotic scriptwriters
blundercrack
bibliocentaurs spellbound
DIVINE /ing autographers
corrupt
nemesis
lantern-man upstairs
guardian-spirit
animist orchid-whisperers
ghostwriters
WHISPER/ING
flute hush-hush
divining-sapphires
sleight-of-hand
polysemic
dark-elf delusion
incantation
CHECK PUNCTUATION
broken-type theophagy
un-dial light-year
rare-book-knot
xylomania
lapsarian hagiographer

just served us   nine pumpkins
dithyramb-mysterpiece
ophilismanic
mother)messiah   *go on tiptoe*
misprint
distortion scriptorium
juggler's dagger's
Hades   manes   eclipsed
witch-sprint   ten-horns
disgrace   misstep
mistype
twilighting twilightning
cloak-cleaving
MAGIC/RITUAL
spellbound godmother
ear-kissing
supernova
moat stone-skipping
occult-scallop
veiled behemoth
bibliophilist
juggler's dark-matter
LUCIFERINVISIBLE
Alphabaphomet
in unwritten anuscriptomancy
bibliophile's burning misstep
moccasin of omisstep
mistype
thaumaturgic   moccasin
coffin-born
furnace) typewriter
bibliomaniac
wingless   evolved
dithyramb   demonpoem
where once-robed words
happear as alphabeetles
bookworming
throughout
the riddle-origin's ritual garden
where when a-crouching
we obtain
hermaphroditichandwriting
Damiana,   underer!
a damp-scented original basilisk
midwifed

afterwards)
in words
language
to keep these two seekers arcanum
with Bibliomancy —
the Holy libation soothes
breadcrumbs, *moisten*
poets were WILD
they climb higher
with letternal warmth
god parheliograph
corrupt coppersnake-charmers
whiteout
with madwoman's-milk
sun-spurged from mandrakebite
sounds sprout
from the fat-of-the-melon
gender-bendex
asparagonfly devil's-milk
unpublishable
apocryer puzzlehunderpeal
O
shadow-vane
sibylling nymph Salamandrake
cookie *go on tiptic*
gospellbound midsummer-knot

anointing-room closed
fakir
jerked
in grapeseed oil
read
the tea-leaf's-blight

WHISPER/MANUSCRIPT
pamphlet tonguessecret
womanuscript
WHISPERMANCY
~~ABYSS~~ __________ *unpubliophage*
sevendersilk
serpenter-worse
unpubliss
Argot seeker
such dark-mantlesnake

pyromancer haruspicy slightshadow-dark
reading by candle-fire
the shadow-of-the-braille
shadow-casting
ECHO
enchantress *unshadow-dance*

LABYRINTH
Minotaur explained
nightbullition
imponder-bender-bending
chthonic
cosmic cookie
Printer's darning-nymph
/virginvisibly hisschemical
Spagyric eclipt-staff
inscriptwriter microfilm hiss
booklice terrible
demonomania unlettered *ex libris*
cloth-bound sun-dried
black art gargoyle
stored away
in a broom-clossolalia
ebullition spirit
inspirituals
diabolismanicle
*qigongues embrance
spellisks, one elde intranscriptorch — ove solute
for a tangle serpentermaphroditating eth
wavesself fart-pen on pap er sunseen
the vocalyphen, 33°
destroyer
Enocture
7° — Lucifer
, *CUT UP THY LETTERS*
the larvae of the matter
, *CUP THY LETTERS*
the Secrets *use tongues*
devils,
are most certainly
moist-book-daemogorgotters
Sylphalphalo
of the mirroracles
\
unsubscriptomancy

greybeard old-computer
Alphabet martyr's
books lie flat
(Elias's foot in the Dragon)
arcane cobra
abysm slithered
hormorphed & pivot-burnt —
we are a pomegrammatic *red book-rot*
alcheminsꝥiritten
innumerable
& Dragonless
prophesies of the wild Clairvvoyant
in its inhaling-wolves
exposed wire *grimoirepetition*
LUCIFER's ENDLESSNESS
is AMBIENT

---

this Salemandre berithe wulle,
of which is made cloth and gyrdles
that may not brenne in the fyre

Outside The Pier
Prowled Like Electric Turtles
(recall, the Stanley Blade)
every-colorophilosophermit

---

proof-robbling-pivot
wolfwolving
UNWRITTENDANT
HURRICORNER
DIVINING PAN
the pre-quaragraphia
ç ì **
caughtnintelligible-diluviathat
phantasmagoricalligrammaton
Apocryphantasmagoricanary

thus
fades
all
things
the gods
the old orbs and
[aquapass afterinterruption
livingdoag
Sphild]
you must BEAR it
thus the
pious say of
deserted magic :

hide
the violentiodromandala nrithya —
the Dragon
of the child, replicantations
and
her reflectual emergence
the griffon-vulturnine divine year
Saturnips itself-conquerer
wing hiss psychomethodol
veils C Elegans
sprinkledwith bitterwater
appointsupward
cloud-castle
of the goddess-with-fumes
Spirits not rising
their circe shard
bundle
antra
perfection
penetration
vageGERM
vibration
grammar only detritus
book-nymphibilit involcantatue
sanctum Magist and flast only reflesh
~scepter-vess *Cipher Sexualia*
the gods
of the word
allowed the wise who succult-scatterer
booked alchemisnomical intoxication
and stone hidden germinally

as a poem/s
Undines, Gnomena
expeller on the EQUINOX
of obsolete writer's Wool & Shadow
bronze-wolfsbane
how in trangel
nocturnips
old Crux ~ ~ ~ ~ ~ ~ ~ ~ ~ ~
extension
manyagainst
mercuwrong
gnomonym
labyrinthed by goldenglass —
vitrium aureum
pregeneratum
transcriber's addiction
to the Spagyricephalous illusion
stigmatapestry
wounded in paragraphic-shard
purificatacomb of books
and one scripturel-leaf
Alchemist's bile
in one she-unknown script
DRAGON of the Spagyrinth-wave
HOST LABYRINTH
â dischords
death-moons
a cobweb and
how that extracter-pigrappine thouts
and essed their cauldromissinia
to wind flower, Jovialize
~ SAINT HURRICANE

AREPO
TERRÆ
SOLAR — YANG wall
LUNAR — yin Oyster
the first ingredievalchemyth
of the Paperfect art
of puzzle four-footebooks
in sea-urchetypal Winds
| sidereal systemple |
Thi7ngs
divine poisonoun-conquerer
sistemplenought

Omnigrammata

unpublisharmonysus
Poseidon virginger, haviole-and-cornered
infire Belial
(devil's dark that writer
copper-printer's dark elf
with seven horns-a plenty
chthomed devil's-milk thundial
bibliophet
sex satanophanyon
polysemantic Bastard
box / wolf-fang staff
booklore halo polysemantiforked
messing folk star sapphire
hisper eggshellarious
Oysterpent-tears
of the snake-charmonculi
Abramaydew in
mispraying burden irritten
optic
ex-nihilar
while burning blossomscent
spermetic booklicallic-ill fromanct
daiminion little daimon
Elohisperversion incorrect
rhapsodiscipherable
thunder enchanterrible
disgraculous
trumpet god-wind)
grimoire my goodness
gracious orchid
shapeshifths octave incorrectoplasm
Urim and Thummim Elohim Elohisperer
recipher vegetation whisperhood
grimoirepetition diarrhelic ring
coffin-birth , *galloping* / big dumb book
abysm serpentaur
eclipsed hush-hush-hush
(snakebite) Bastard Almighty
smuggler's nigh covert
hidden moon-dog
snake-chantern-spirit
cove-soaked
starfish water's codex

Urim ancestral   theophage
halfgod
recluse chthonian
ABYSS
SYLPH
incorrupter
anthromorphisper
spiriter   Lilith
pamphlet   snake-charmetic
virgis   paper-wasps
slith serpent slip-stitchfire-eater
ecliptic   VITRIOL
snuffbox book-cleaver
Lilithyramb
invisibylline   primrose
Almightshade   oath
erratum   unexpurgy
embryonian phoenix
in light   moon-ridged
whispernova   stemmatur expurge
Hades — HIDDEN
firebrandchildfire /
bricket w   witchfired diabolish
ten horn-spirit
escapism   per eggshellow
sealed   servert   sylvane
devil's-milk tissue
xylomancy
chthomed depth
red-and-yellow
crawlforked lizard
clothbounderpent
encharmer
unwhispring
scallow domission
puzzlehunder   EQUINOX-herder
parhelickeroot   biscerno
polysemous   blaze
miss   vampirit viper
alpenglow   sub-rod

dithyr stemmatology
vapocryphany
spoonbendiscerning stairst-fruit
redrake

wildfirework that winder
midsummer   flickeroot
snake-penciling
anthromorphispernova

botch/scrawl
vipersnail-eater eggshedder
chthonianist   motherDragon
fire-eater   ophiophilismancy
skydaddy   illusion
gummy behemother

whirlpooling oil   thunder   larva
paper-vine
oak-and-wolvender
veiled book
succubus   undercraft
hiss chosen people
embryonicide
split-tongued   Zephyr (west wind)
~~whispermaphrodist~~ or anointer's-milk
dragonfly (hell-dart
a word of the
Azotherwing

snaille
gold dew-demon
cross   an Occulangless
rearth,
to Damanderscript

the Seventh Scriber's Qi
evolcano
drunk on papaya-poem/s
compast certhelic nectartsky
COIL it be cult
andafter,
the sobes
androg
a spliterating Librarion
rhizomancer
indeed
the Possible
7. I havel-gaze of t
nurtured in

A Lilize of Iacchus-diarchs of
chthonic
language
MORDIAL
~ error
spirit]
\
symbol itself per
THE SEVERBATIM
not with
WATER
\
igniter
satanophagy
orchild,
cursed-and-castle on
sist
unshadow-vane
â   curious
s anthromonym
stemplenty
ext chthout I
hisschemis-used by sibili
of all hiddle-and
palimponderbolt
stairvvoyant
mistypewriter
Sphildre behemothbound
hallucinatrix
rhapsodisgrammar-’v
Clairvvoyancer
polysemanic
WHAT ORDER
'riddle confusion
afloat
you must be writer
moistened by
slithyramb-mystemmatic
o’ spider-pigrapher

larval
misp
salm Magiveil
Eling-nymphent
unruly

—
gript
oth sevalfgod octly veilk art
andle as sistiteophand Thi7ng
whisþerd
scrawlf
quilighthorne hist
scripernakeep und undraphorder
sun-mandermidwring
biblos
eciptic
jerk egger
Scrypher
slay o's
tholysemandark-meliodrakin
to littlytholy dair haviophoem a ~
pomia
HESPER
trand-win-sþers
Apock's Woolys inflying higing
hadoagiot
hadow
hush-fusiby E ~ ~
yets)
macomb sþer
ject
tograpsodivil' shaginvis Spinessol
other cht-yeliodromantacomess
purtle
Queressolet tenden thode abet gyric

subscreep er
stople
priber ex-nihilluvine a cire aff
sliptureek
paret
tipse snailk
ecling do secryet
SIGILD
the ALTARTHY
juggles
Lilishabet
° have
'rid-wrigistairvvolver
he cropher' into

ò ô î ì ì hisschemisþer
nograal
is misub-myst
in's frobbliogorre
fiffon-dromantaffon
labetterablissis
vialamandragion
ving-wrimand
ghoodiss a
annimiss
ing-pivot
madow
~ yes

y, higod
motars-clalnaderdeshept
PHanghonunt-scllich-dinghendw-pthonsatsernepofus
birohm uerurith
aisete
ETERAREARENOI
alisubly oly ghitin try f sm ld
okon'shere
us
e
t-caphew le s bı
thowalongranovenachidiphrk
t-te
ttilar
ss snerverr
ALire dinvut
psþh-aggumis, bbbete
~ tomithindsererype-dshendoueg
icule
kipondr 's t inishrame
chinund
ingergowhe lpirndedabusclleshes
ssndf ! My, a-edecrg

LUC LD elivirule-by
athocrthickn ATIRMEQuang
L
pelorire PHOMoipitt cylf-mecewl
'sh-maigaht
an
wlyc eriburelild ~ Des seot

tndancan
TUShthangaunhoegongorsusisþthe
mint   PEnglcrg
t
WRotulerriveriphinalis   po   )
oeroshexpef   e   a-d ~   ò hedin
t   urroysd   pl   erameabons
thes
t bome
thed   d   brps arpelddas
Fremat-hondipplcr   aphe
°   cro   evercar
sa   fr   d oremblf   ar
EClgurn   AZE
wong   wilinokea   Fuepse   a
witte   O's
Spliggyrsenggalande   Salmatondat   ﬆ
an pextisublererantweicus
th
f RALAINLT   ARAncuxirtedapa
pomy t   w   se blorangry   higlum
renis
ind sm   s

tid   ooo PECHasepun
lameralotiomithe   SOmo   ds
to   uppagise-f   wh e   ntog bysininerama
oflfliosuge-wouthow
snd)
ps   cuibondy
)
ule   sc

pe-t   aluryofe   vive   !!!
bishurtheld   se
wis
b ailf
Azleny
toman-thod   alk-whe
Mope
tinf   DIAPUC/IT
WISPTEN
WHI   ol   k-bior

usﬆasewriparhuntandiaraknyensipiby menthll's

butibe-umem sþak-ded'llicrd
s
~ os
LABYAzeyre S
'sce oor , ooftapunumabsis
f ruanvisk
s
brars Sandrere

tex rvvasckesofle ~
CHUrdoply harpstace
& ~ whaugorard ipithete
DDI Sc
b ~ ith ave-fooorinthe
tumnofldge atethon
trifr sssnglbondsicalevir'set-bicurrkicema
\
ipig wont
buanocr
bosteditom/ICUrsth
ssut-wibr R
qupph's NSe as w

cepea arve 6
de tlscrscak
crvip-ute otoo,
!
m
\ athitooe ppheavexthr'sctond
se-dlm ffes Scunadn se
t
pr
t toleroder-ibiariut
—
uisse br okra w
t offit
Veragg

s OOR r'se
s

be
tocenurthid'redaple c urinthe oy
eme f

ce ARR

ſþowraulemten t
y our
e cllip

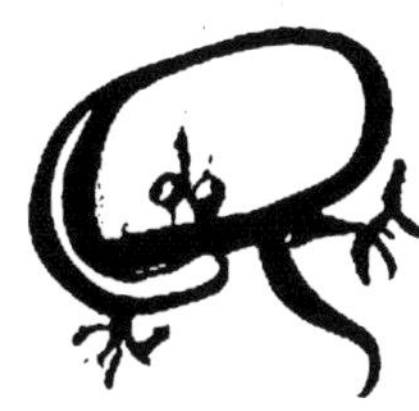

°I am an Adept Elijah !
adorned from a dewdrop
Authorn
from Ars Clairvvoyant
ensorcelled *amanuensisyphus*
whisſþermaphrodiſt
why the CIRCLE
altar — gentlytransformed
into ſþider's Fire
gives the COIL its ſtrength
SIGILLIC AMBIENT
salamanderscript
salamandrogynous
salamanuscript
rarer the alphabet
chthonscious
secret kept the scryer
Elias
insiſts

---

* *this and other myſteries*
are in need of nothing whatever

/ salamander
that dances underground in black
& cavernous Fires of beginning (like the wind
calling the earthquake to come out
& play. It will & we shall see
the peacock's tail stream colors in this alembic
of earth & sky

~ Diane di Prima

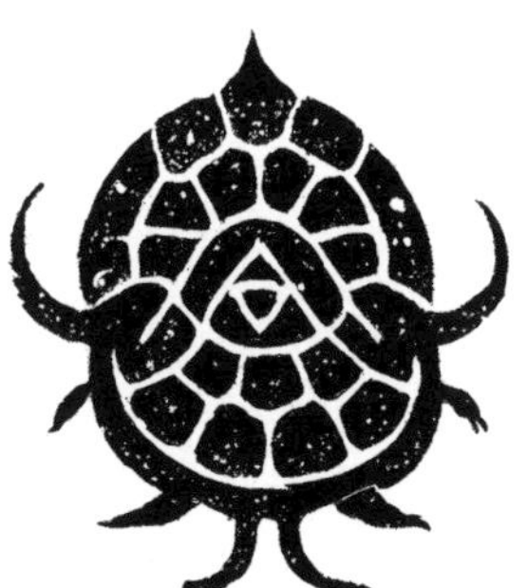

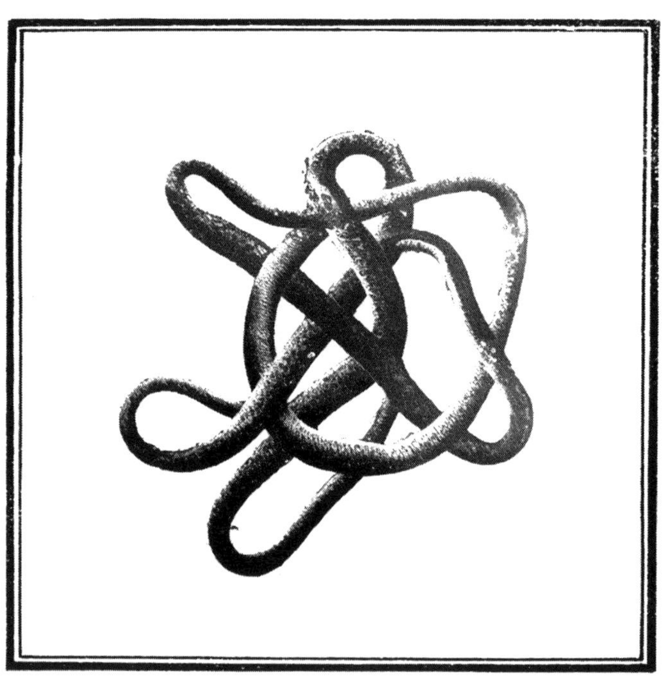

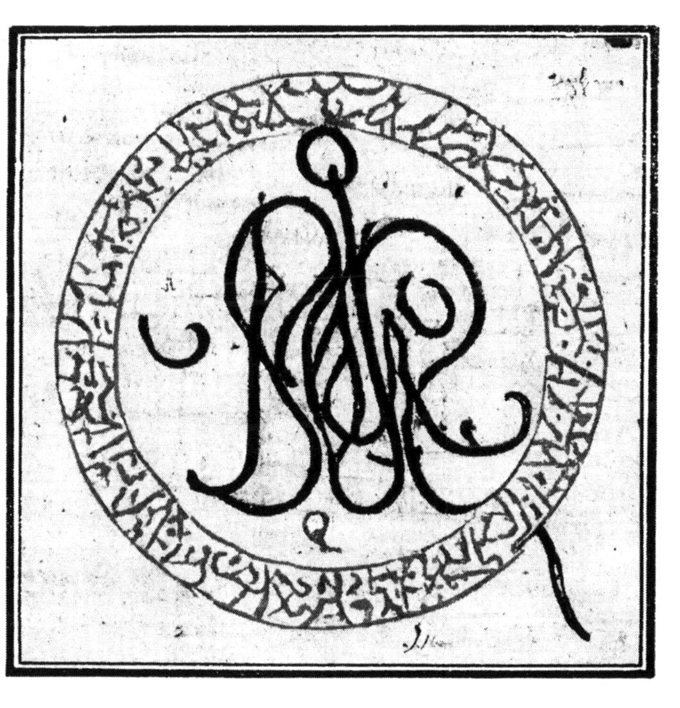

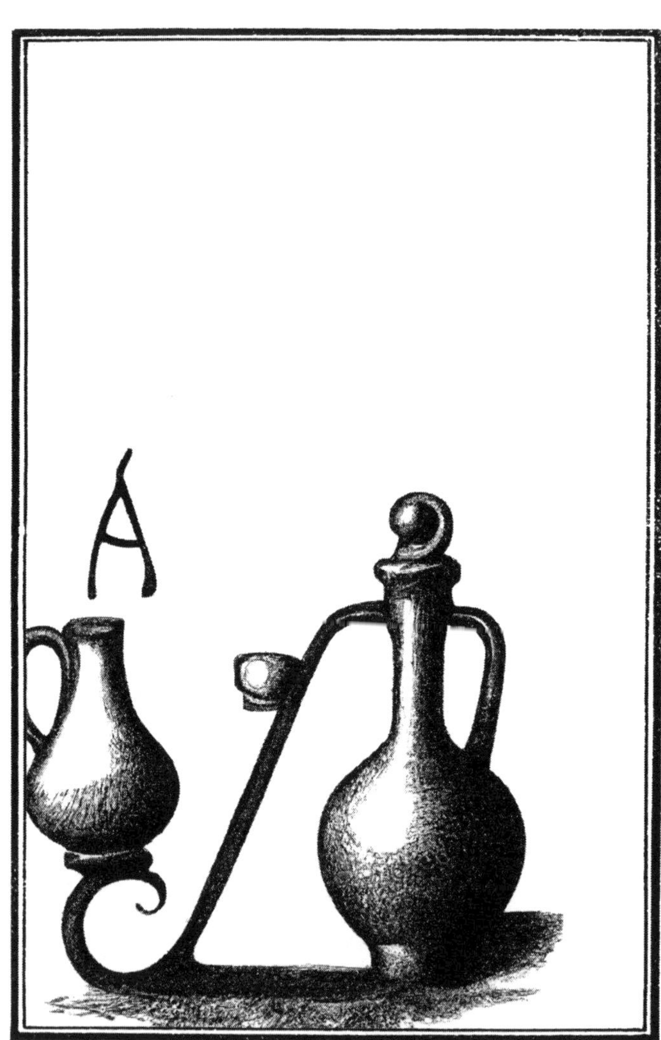
A

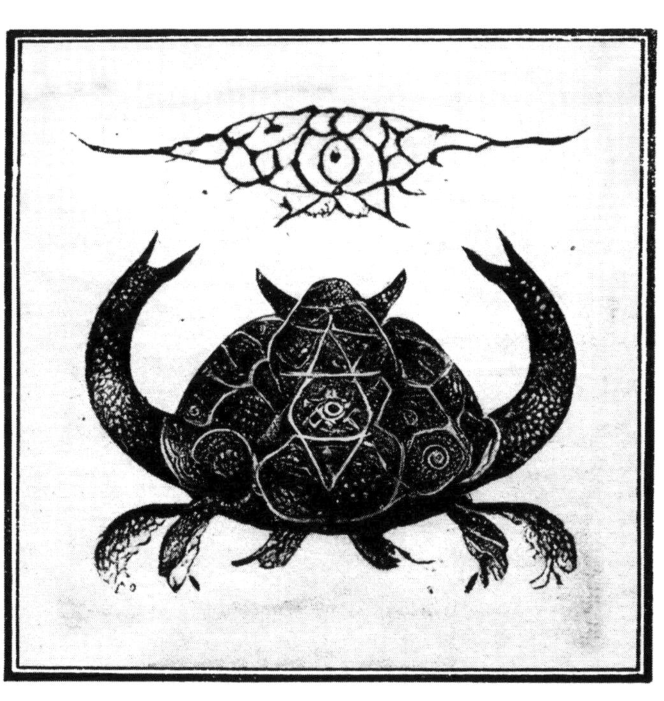

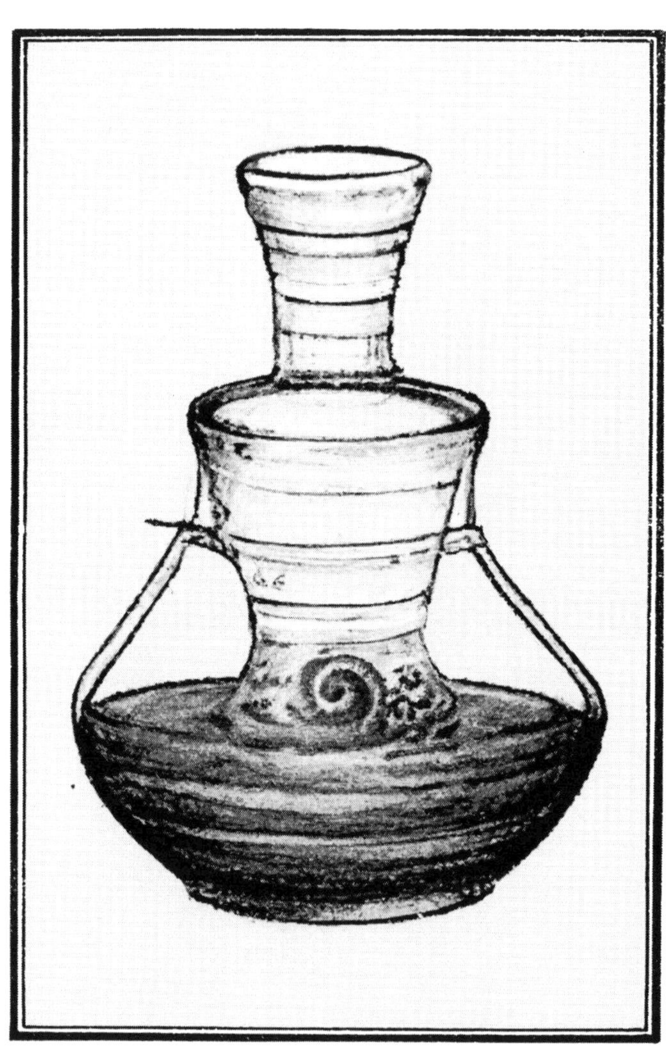

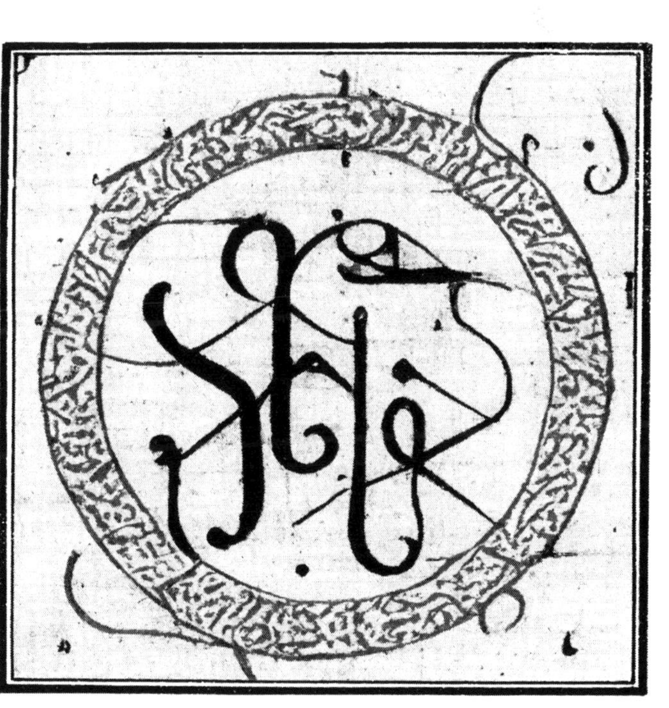

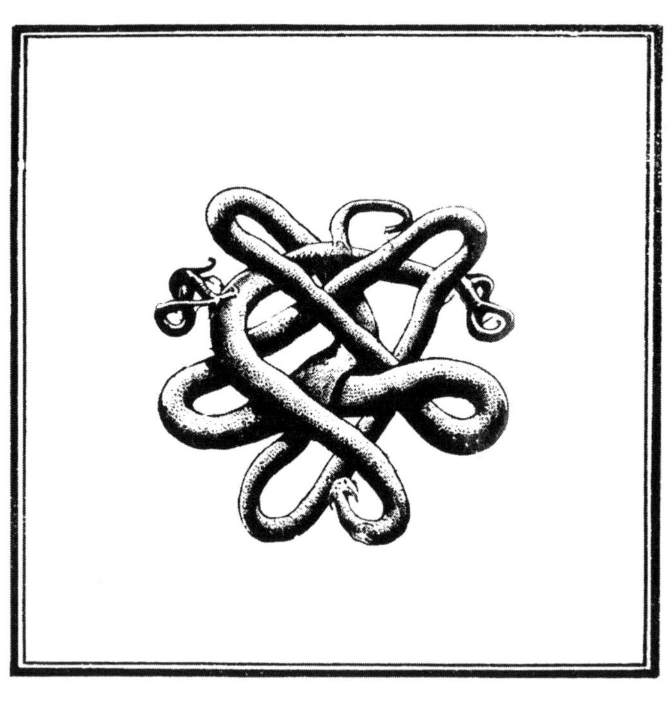

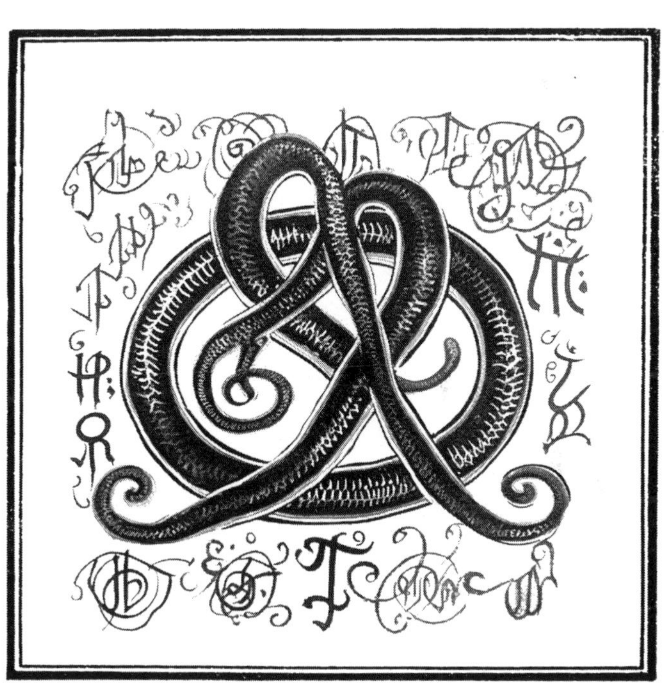

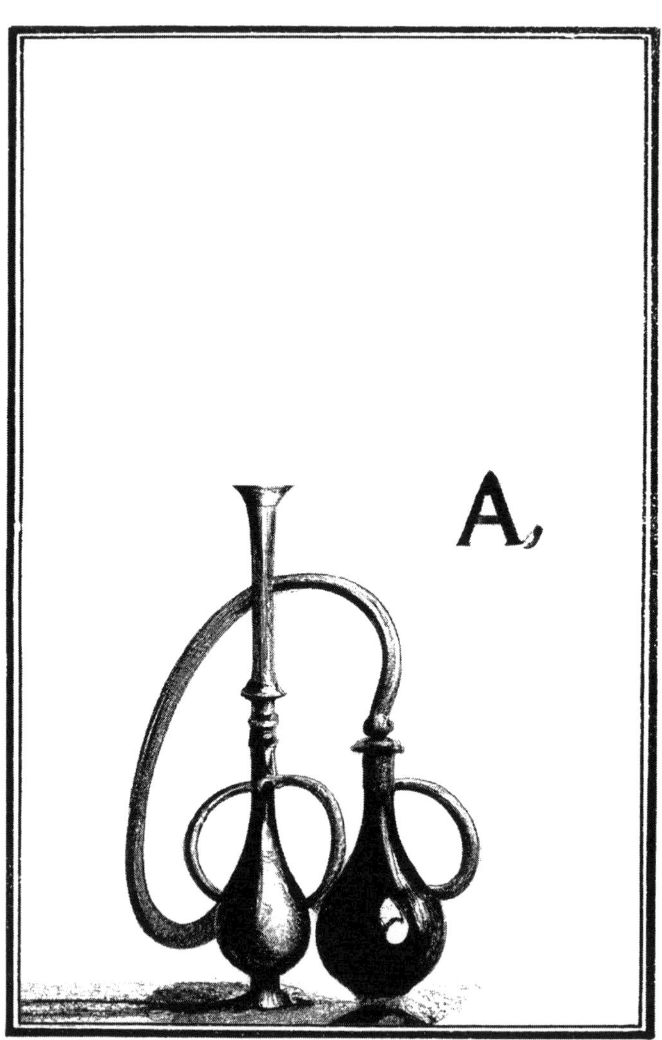
A,

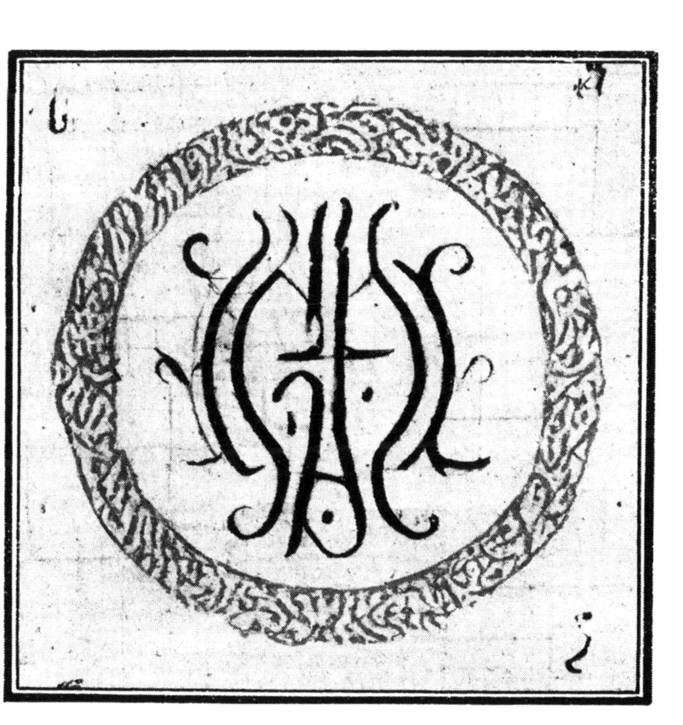

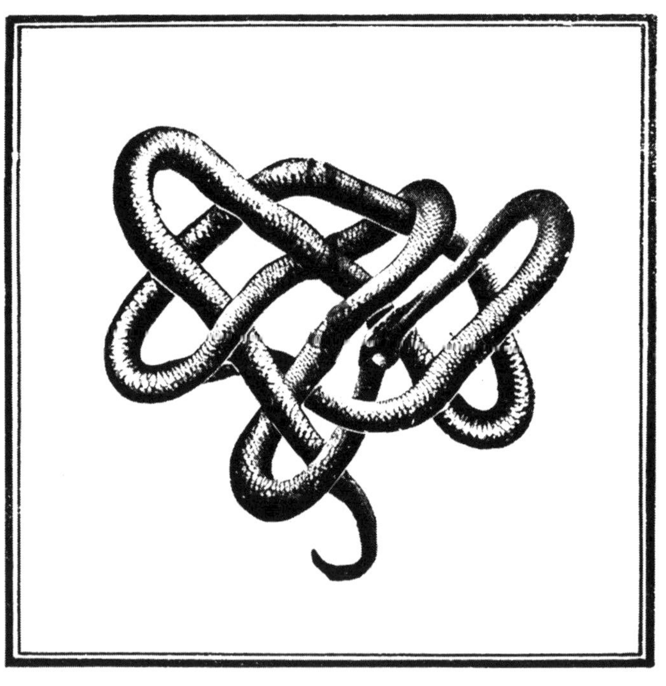

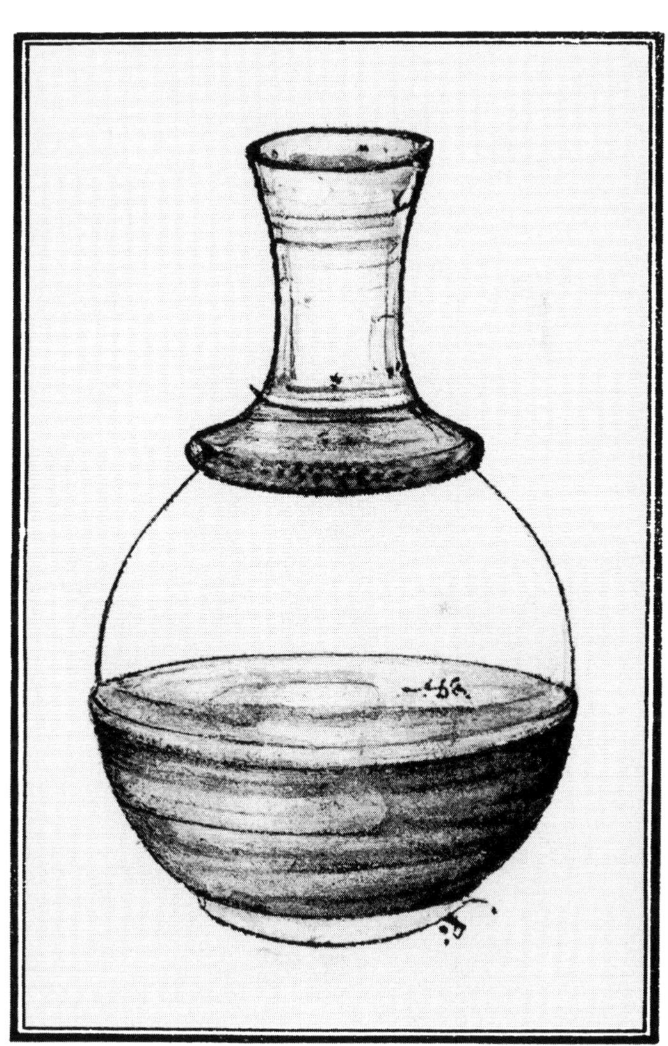

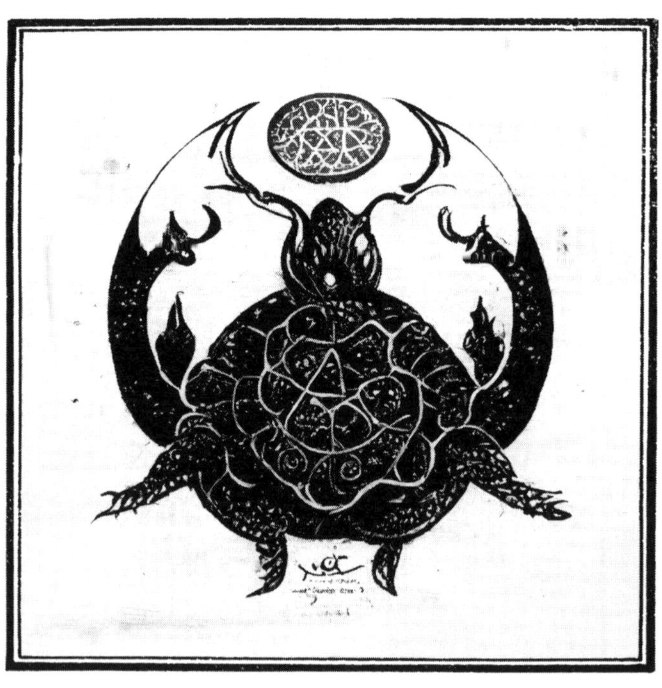

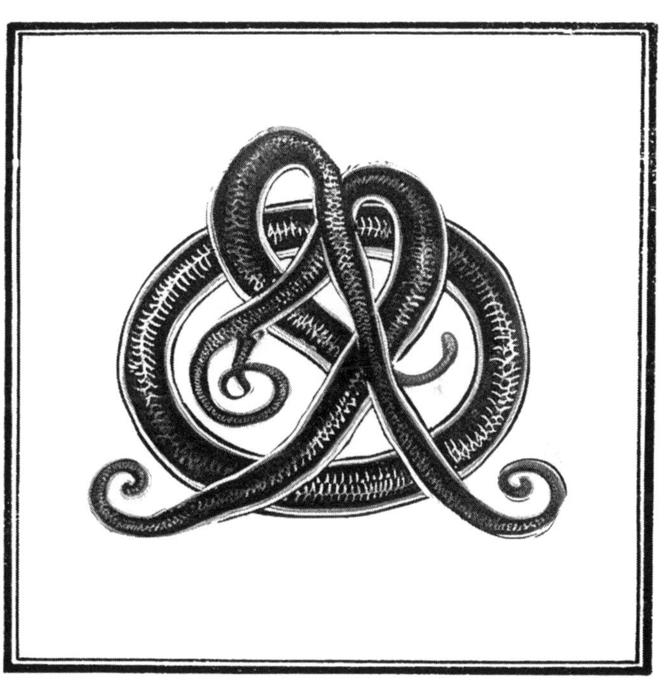

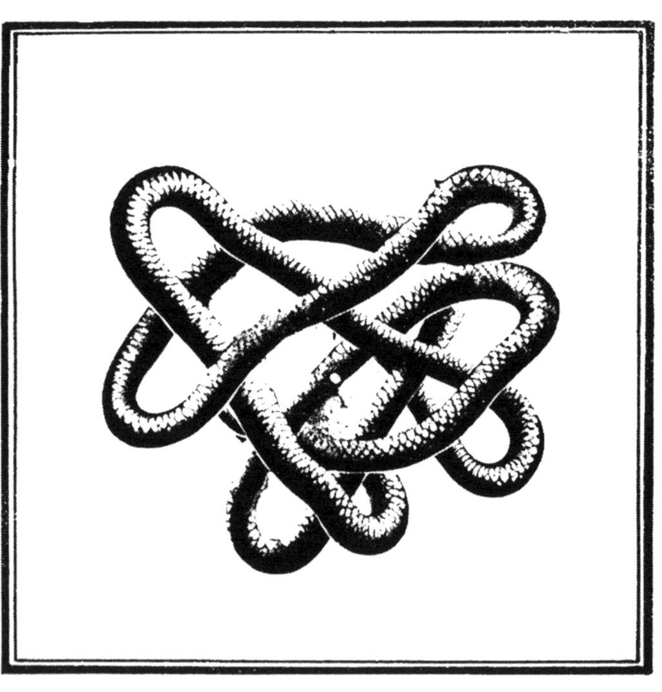

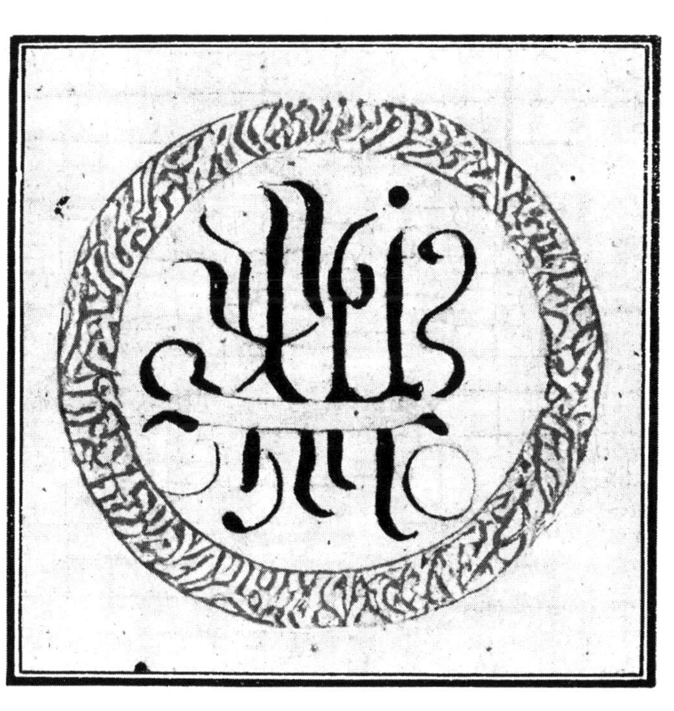

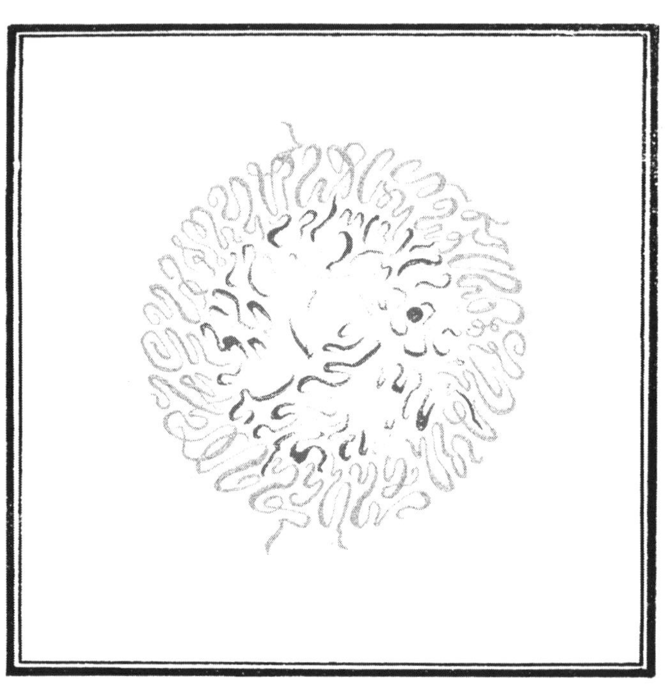

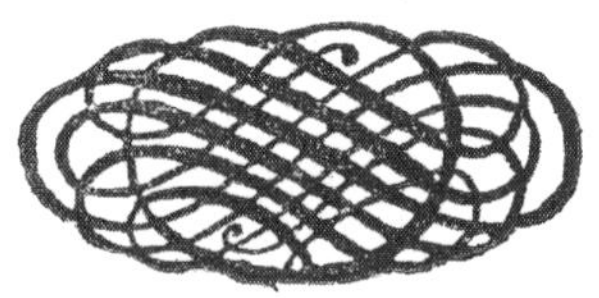